The Essence of Croatia : A Travel Preparation Guide

Alexander Becker

All rights reserved. No part of this publication may be reproduced, distributed, or transmitted in any form or by any means, including photocopying, recording, or other electronic or mechanical methods, without the prior written permission of the publisher, except in the case of brief quotations embodied in critical reviews and certain other noncommercial uses permitted by copyright law.

Copyright © (Alexander Becker) (2023).

Alexander Becker	1
INTRODUCTION	7
CHAPTER ONE	9
Introduction to Croatia	9
•Welcome to Croatia	9
•Geography and Climate	12
•Cultural Background and History	16
CHAPTER TWO	**21**
Planning Your Trip	21
•Best Time to Visit Croatia	21
•Visa and Travel Requirements	25
•Budgeting and Currency	30
•Transportation Options	36
CHAPTER THREE	**43**
Top Destinations	43
•Zagreb - The Capital City	43
Must-Visit Attractions	47
Dining and Nightlife	52
• Dubrovnik - The Pearl of the Adriatic	57
Exploring the Old Town	62
Game of Thrones Filming Locations	68
•Split - Ancient History and Modern Vibes	72
Diocletian's Palace	77
Nearby Islands and Beaches	82
•Plitvice Lakes National Park	86
Natural Wonders of Plitvice	91

Hiking and Wildlife Viewing	97
CHAPTER FOUR	**103**
Hidden Gems and Off-the-Beaten-Path	103
•Istrian Peninsula	103
Pula - Roman Amphitheater	108
Rovinj - Charming Coastal Town	112
•Zadar	117
Sea Organ and Sun Salutation	122
Historic Sites and Museums	128
•Korcula Island	131
Marco Polo's Birthplace	137
Wine Tasting and Beaches	141
CHAPTER FIVE	**145**
Croatia's Culinary Delights	145
• Traditional Dishes and Cuisine	145
•Popular Restaurants and Local Eateries	149
•Wine Regions and Tastings	153
CHAPTER SIX	**159**
Outdoor Activities and Adventures	159
• Sailing the Adriatic Coast	159
•Hiking and Trekking Trails	164
•Water Sports and Diving	169
CHAPTER SEVEN	**175**
Cultural Experiences and Festivals	175
• Croatian Folklore and Traditions	175
• Music and Dance Festivals	180
• Carnival Celebrations	184
CHAPTER EIGHT	**191**
Practical Tips for Travelers	191

- Language and Communication — 191
- Safety and Emergency Information — 196
- Local Customs and Etiquette — 200

CHAPTER NINE — 205

Sustainable Travel and Responsible Tourism 205

- Eco-Friendly Practices in Croatia — 205
- Supporting Local Communities — 209

CHAPTER TEN — 215

Useful Phrases and Vocabulary — 215

- Basic Croatian Phrases for Travelers — 215
- Food and Restaurant Vocabulary — 219

CHAPTER ELEVEN — 225

- Conclusion — 225

INTRODUCTION

Welcome to the breathtaking land of Croatia, a hidden gem nestled at the crossroads of Central Europe and the Adriatic Sea. With its stunning coastline, ancient history, and vibrant culture, Croatia has emerged as a captivating destination for travelers seeking both natural beauty and rich heritage. From the sun-kissed beaches and picturesque islands of the Dalmatian coast to the historic cities brimming with medieval charm, Croatia offers an unforgettable journey that caters to every traveler's desires.

Embark on a voyage through time as you explore well-preserved Roman ruins, medieval fortresses, and Baroque architecture. Lose yourself in the narrow cobblestone streets of Dubrovnik, stroll along the ancient walls that guard its secrets, and immerse yourself in the ambiance of a living museum. Traverse the narrow alleys of Split and encounter the magnificent Diocletian's Palace, an awe-inspiring blend of ancient history and modern life.

For nature enthusiasts, Croatia's rugged landscapes offer a playground of adventure. Discover the cascading waterfalls of Plitvice Lakes National Park, where emerald-green lakes interlace with wooden footbridges and lush greenery. Escape to the captivating beauty of Krka National Park, where waterfalls cascade over limestone cliffs into crystal-clear pools.

However, Croatia's most alluring allure lies along its sun-drenched coastline and over a thousand enchanting islands. Sail the azure waters of the Adriatic, where you'll find a hidden paradise around every bend. From the glamorous shores of Hvar to the unspoiled tranquility of Vis, each island boasts its own unique charm and captivating history.

Indulge in Croatia's delectable cuisine, a mouthwatering fusion of Mediterranean and Eastern European influences. Savor the taste of freshly caught seafood, homemade olive oil, and local wines that have been perfected through generations.

Whether you seek adventure, relaxation, or cultural enrichment, Croatia offers an unforgettable tapestry of experiences. Join us as we unveil the secrets of this captivating country, where every step reveals a new chapter in an age-old story. Get ready to be swept away by the magic of Croatia, where past and present intertwine to create an experience like no other. So, pack your bags, and let Croatia cast its spell on you as we embark on an unforgettable journey together.

CHAPTER ONE

Introduction to Croatia

•*Welcome to Croatia*

Nestled in the heart of Europe, Croatia is a picturesque gem that beckons travelers with its stunning landscapes, historical charm, and azure Adriatic coastline. This vibrant country offers a unique blend of ancient history, rich culture, delectable cuisine, and natural wonders, making it a dream destination for travelers seeking diverse experiences. Whether you're an adventure enthusiast, a history buff, a nature lover, or simply looking to unwind in idyllic settings, Croatia has something to offer for everyone.

Discovering Croatia's Cities
- Dubrovnik: Often referred to as the "Pearl of the Adriatic," Dubrovnik's fortified walls, ancient buildings, and cobblestone streets exude medieval charm. Explore the Old Town, stroll along the city walls, and enjoy breathtaking views of the Adriatic Sea.

- Split: Home to the majestic Diocletian's Palace, a UNESCO World Heritage Site, Split is a city that seamlessly blends history with a vibrant modern atmosphere. Wander through the narrow alleys, visit impressive museums, and relax in lively cafes along the waterfront.

- Zagreb: Croatia's capital city, Zagreb, is a hub of culture, art, and entertainment. Explore the Upper Town's historic landmarks, like St. Mark's Church and the Zagreb Cathedral, and indulge in the city's thriving food and nightlife scene.

Exploring Nature's Bounty
- Plitvice Lakes National Park: A natural wonderland, Plitvice Lakes boasts a cascading series of turquoise lakes and waterfalls surrounded by lush forests. Wander through wooden walkways and bridges to experience this UNESCO-listed park up close.

- Krka National Park: Another jewel in Croatia's crown, Krka National Park features ethereal waterfalls, tranquil lakes, and abundant flora and fauna. Take a refreshing swim beneath the cascades and bask in the park's serene beauty.

- Hvar Island: Known for its lavender fields and pristine beaches, Hvar is a haven for nature enthusiasts. Explore charming towns, vineyards, and olive groves, or take a boat to discover hidden coves and secluded bays.

Immersing in Croatia's Culture
- Festivals and Celebrations: Embrace Croatia's lively spirit by participating in colorful festivals

such as the Dubrovnik Summer Festival, the Špancirfest in Varaždin, and the International Folklore Festival in Zagreb.

- Cuisine and Wine: Delight your taste buds with traditional Croatian dishes like peka (slow-cooked meat and vegetables), pasticada (beef stew), and seafood delights along the coast. Don't forget to sample local wines from vineyards across the country.

Adventure and Activities
- Island Hopping: With over a thousand islands, Croatia invites you to hop on a ferry and explore its diverse island offerings. Each island boasts its own unique character and attractions.

- Water Sports: From snorkeling and scuba diving in crystal-clear waters to kayaking along the stunning coastline, Croatia offers a plethora of water-based activities for adventure seekers.

- Trekking and Hiking: Lace up your boots and embark on hiking trails that wind through mountains, forests, and coastal cliffs, providing awe-inspiring vistas at every turn.

Conclusion:
Croatia's irresistible charm lies in its ability to cater to various travel interests. Whether you are fascinated by history and architecture, captivated by nature's beauty, intrigued by local culture, or

eager to indulge in thrilling adventures, Croatia promises an unforgettable journey. So, pack your bags and let Croatia weave its magic on your heart as you create cherished memories that will last a lifetime.

•*Geography and Climate*

Nestled in the heart of Europe, Croatia is a country of stunning natural beauty, rich cultural heritage, and diverse landscapes. With its diverse geographical features, ranging from the sun-kissed coastline along the Adriatic Sea to the majestic mountains in the interior, Croatia offers an unforgettable experience for travelers seeking adventure, history, and relaxation. In this travel guide, we will delve into the fascinating geography and climate of Croatia, providing essential information to help you plan your dream vacation to this enchanting destination.

1. Geography of Croatia:

1.1. Location and Borders:
Croatia is located in the southeastern part of Europe, bordering Slovenia to the northwest, Hungary to the northeast, Serbia to the east, Bosnia and Herzegovina to the southeast, and Montenegro to the south. Its western edge is caressed by the crystal-clear waters of the Adriatic Sea.

1.2. Dalmatian Coast:
The Dalmatian Coast, stretching from Istria in the north to Dubrovnik in the south, is one of Croatia's most iconic regions. It boasts a series of beautiful islands, charming coastal towns, and pristine beaches. Notable cities along the coast include Split, Zadar, and Sibenik, each with its unique historical and cultural landmarks.

1.3. Istria and the Kvarner Region:
Istria, the largest Croatian peninsula, is a verdant paradise famous for its picturesque hilltop villages, vineyards, and olive groves. The Kvarner Region, including the islands of Krk and Cres, offers a blend of scenic landscapes and coastal resorts, making it a favored destination for nature lovers and beachgoers alike.

1.4. Inland Croatia:
The inland regions of Croatia are dominated by the Dinaric Alps, a rugged mountain range that stretches parallel to the Adriatic Sea. Plitvice Lakes National Park, a UNESCO World Heritage site, is a stunning collection of cascading waterfalls, turquoise lakes, and lush forests located in this area.

1.5. Central Croatia and Slavonia:
Central Croatia is characterized by rolling hills, picturesque villages, and historic towns like Zagreb, the capital city. On the other hand, Slavonia, in the

east, is an agricultural region known for its vast plains and traditional culture.

2. *Climate of Croatia:*

2.1. Mediterranean Climate:
The coastal regions of Croatia, including the Dalmatian Coast and parts of the Istrian Peninsula, experience a Mediterranean climate. Summers are hot and dry, with average temperatures ranging from 25°C to 35°C (77°F to 95°F). Winters are mild, with temperatures seldom dropping below 10°C (50°F).

2.2. Continental Climate:
Inland Croatia, including Zagreb and parts of Slavonia, features a continental climate. Summers are warm and sunny, with average temperatures ranging from 20°C to 30°C (68°F to 86°F). Winters are colder, with temperatures often dipping below freezing, and snow is common in higher elevations.

2.3. Mountain Climate:
The Dinaric Alps in the central and southern parts of the country experience a mountain climate. Summers are mild and refreshing, making it a pleasant escape from the coastal heat. However, winters can be harsh, with heavy snowfall and temperatures well below freezing.

2.4. Adriatic Sea:

The Adriatic Sea's influence moderates the coastal regions' temperatures, creating a pleasant maritime climate. The sea temperature ranges from around 12°C (54°F) in winter to 25°C (77°F) in summer, making it ideal for swimming and water sports during the warmer months.

3. Best Time to Visit:

The best time to visit Croatia depends on your preferences and the experiences you seek:

3.1. Summer (June to August):
Summer is the peak tourist season when Croatia comes alive with festivals, events, and vibrant beach scenes. The coastal areas are bustling with tourists, and the sea is warm and inviting for swimming. However, expect higher accommodation prices and crowded attractions during this time.

3.2. Spring (April to May) and Autumn (September to October):
These shoulder seasons are ideal for travelers seeking a balance between pleasant weather and fewer crowds. The temperatures are milder, making it more comfortable for exploring historical sites and engaging in outdoor activities.

3.3. Winter (November to March):
Winter is the offseason in Croatia, especially in the coastal regions, where many hotels and restaurants may close temporarily. However, if you enjoy

winter sports or want to experience the magical charm of snowy landscapes, consider visiting the inland and mountainous areas during this time.

Croatia's diverse geography and climate offer a myriad of experiences for every traveler. From the breathtaking coastline and historic cities to the tranquil islands and majestic mountains, Croatia's beauty and charm will leave an indelible mark on your heart. Whether you're an adventure enthusiast, history buff, or a sun-seeking beach lover, Croatia has something to offer you year-round. So, pack your bags and get ready for an unforgettable journey through this enchanting destination.

Remember to respect the local culture, protect the environment, and immerse yourself in the unique experiences that Croatia has to offer. Enjoy your journey, and may your Croatian adventure be filled with cherished memories and captivating moments!

•*Cultural Background and History*

Croatia, nestled along the stunning Adriatic coast, is a country with a rich cultural background and history that dates back thousands of years. As you embark on a journey to this enchanting destination, prepare to be captivated by its diverse heritage, ancient architecture, and breathtaking landscapes.

This travel guide aims to provide you with a comprehensive overview of Croatia's cultural tapestry, shedding light on its historical milestones, traditional customs, arts, cuisine, and the unique blend of influences that have shaped this Mediterranean gem.

1. Geographical and Historical Overview:

Croatia's strategic location at the crossroads of Central Europe, the Mediterranean, and the Balkans has significantly influenced its history. The region was inhabited by various tribes and civilizations, including the Illyrians, Romans, Slavs, and Venetians. By the 7th century, Croats settled in the area, and the Kingdom of Croatia emerged.

In the medieval period, Croatia became a prominent European kingdom and enjoyed flourishing cultural and economic ties with neighboring countries. The influence of the Roman Catholic Church and Venetian Republic was instrumental in shaping Croatia's art, architecture, and culture.

2. Cultural Influences and Diversity:

Croatia's cultural heritage is an intriguing blend of different influences, owing to its tumultuous past and geographical location. Northern regions bear traces of Central European traditions, while the coastal areas boast a strong Mediterranean flair.

The influences of neighboring countries, such as Italy, Hungary, and Turkey, are also evident in Croatia's cuisine, language, and architecture.

3. Traditional Arts and Crafts:

Croatia's traditional arts and crafts have been passed down through generations, showcasing the nation's creativity and craftsmanship. From intricate lace-making in the northern town of Lepoglava to the vibrant, hand-painted pottery in Dubrovnik and Korčula, each region boasts its unique artistic expression. The Klis Fortress hosts annual sword-dancing festivals that hark back to medieval times, offering a glimpse into Croatia's martial traditions.

4. Architecture and Historical Landmarks:

Croatia is home to a plethora of architectural gems that narrate the country's history. The historic city of Dubrovnik, known as the "Pearl of the Adriatic," features magnificent medieval walls, Baroque churches, and elegant palaces. Split boasts the UNESCO-listed Diocletian's Palace, an ancient Roman palace complex that has been seamlessly integrated into the fabric of the modern city. Zagreb, the capital, showcases a mix of Austro-Hungarian architecture and contemporary design.

5. Festivals and Celebrations:

Participating in Croatia's festivals and celebrations is a fantastic way to immerse yourself in the local culture. Witness the vibrant spectacle of Carnival in Rijeka, where parades, masquerades, and music take over the streets. Experience the rich folklore and traditional dances at the International Folklore Festival in Zagreb, which attracts performers from around the world.

6. Cuisine and Culinary Traditions:

Croatian cuisine is a delightful fusion of Mediterranean and Continental influences, characterized by fresh ingredients and hearty flavors. The coastal regions boast delectable seafood dishes like black risotto, grilled fish, and octopus salad. Inland, indulge in succulent roasted meats, truffles, and štrukli, a traditional pastry filled with cottage cheese. Don't forget to try the local wines and rakija (fruit brandy) for an authentic gastronomic experience.

7. Language and Communication:

The Croatian language is an integral part of the country's cultural identity. Though English is widely spoken in tourist areas, learning a few basic Croatian phrases will endear you to the locals and enhance your travel experience.

8. Music and Dance:

Croatian music and dance traditions reflect the country's regional diversity. The coastal areas are renowned for their klapa singing, a UNESCO-protected form of a cappella singing that celebrates the Adriatic Sea. Inland regions showcase lively folk music accompanied by traditional instruments like the tamburica. Witnessing a traditional Croatian dance performance is an excellent way to feel the rhythm of the nation's cultural heartbeat.

Croatia's cultural background and history are the threads that weave together the tapestry of this captivating country. As you explore its ancient cities, picturesque islands, and stunning landscapes, you'll encounter a unique blend of influences that have shaped Croatia into the mesmerizing destination it is today. Embrace the warmth of its people, savor its diverse cuisine, and immerse yourself in the rich cultural traditions that make Croatia a truly unforgettable travel experience.

CHAPTER TWO

Planning Your Trip

•*Best Time to Visit Croatia*

Croatia, nestled in the heart of Europe along the stunning Adriatic coast, is a destination that captivates visitors with its rich history, diverse landscapes, and vibrant culture. From ancient walled cities to idyllic islands and picturesque national parks, Croatia offers a plethora of experiences for travelers. One of the key factors that can significantly enhance your trip is the timing of your visit. The climate and events throughout the year greatly impact your travel experience. In this comprehensive travel guide, we will explore the best time to visit Croatia, taking into account weather conditions, tourist crowds, local festivals, and more.

1. Spring (March to May):

Spring is one of the most pleasant times to visit Croatia. As the temperatures start to rise, the country comes alive with blossoming flowers and lush greenery. The weather is generally mild, with daytime temperatures ranging from 15°C to 20°C

(59°F to 68°F). This period is perfect for exploring the cities, coastal towns, and national parks without being overwhelmed by the summer crowds.

Highlights:
- Witness the spectacular Plitvice Lakes National Park as the waterfalls gush with melting snow.
- Visit Dubrovnik and Split, exploring their historic old towns without the overwhelming tourist crowds.
- Attend the Easter celebrations in various cities, experiencing the local traditions and customs.

2. *Summer (June to August):*

Summer is undoubtedly the peak tourist season in Croatia, and for good reason. The weather is warm and sunny, with temperatures ranging from 25°C to 30°C (77°F to 86°F) or even higher. The coastal areas, especially the islands, become a hub for beach lovers, yachters, and party-goers.

Highlights:
- Enjoy the lively atmosphere of Hvar, known for its vibrant nightlife and beautiful beaches.
- Experience the International Folklore Festival in Zagreb, a celebration of traditional music and dance.
- Participate in water sports and activities on the stunning beaches of the Dalmatian coast.

3. *Autumn (September to November):*

Autumn is another excellent time to visit Croatia, especially for those seeking a more tranquil and authentic experience. The summer crowds start to disperse, and the weather remains pleasant, with temperatures ranging from 15°C to 25°C (59°F to 77°F). The vineyards are ready for harvest, and it's a great time to explore the culinary delights of the country.

Highlights:
- Attend the grape harvest festivals in Istria and Dalmatia, celebrating Croatia's wine-making heritage.
- Explore the charming Istrian hilltop towns such as Motovun and Grožnjan without the tourist rush.
- Visit the island of Korčula, the reputed birthplace of Marco Polo, and enjoy its peaceful ambiance.

4. Winter (December to February):

Winter in Croatia offers a unique experience, particularly for travelers who appreciate a more laid-back atmosphere and want to avoid the crowds. The coastal regions experience milder winters, with temperatures ranging from 5°C to 15°C (41°F to 59°F), while inland areas can get much colder.

Highlights:

- Experience the magical Advent season in Zagreb, where the city transforms with Christmas markets and festive decorations.
- Explore the historical city of Rovinj, with fewer tourists and a quieter ambiance.
- Hit the slopes in the Platak and Bjelolasica ski resorts, offering winter sports and activities.

5. Shoulder Seasons:

The shoulder seasons, which fall between the peak and off-peak periods, are considered some of the best times to visit Croatia. These include April to early June and September to October. During these months, the weather is generally pleasant, and tourist numbers are lower compared to the peak summer months. This allows for a more enjoyable and authentic experience while still enjoying outdoor activities and festivals.

Croatia is a diverse and captivating destination that offers something for every type of traveler. Determining the best time to visit depends on your preferences, whether you seek warm summer beaches, tranquil autumn landscapes, or festive winter experiences. Consider your interests and priorities when planning your trip to Croatia. Whether you decide to visit during the bustling summer months or opt for the more peaceful shoulder seasons, Croatia's beauty and charm are sure to leave a lasting impression on your journey.

•*Visa and Travel Requirements*

Welcome to Croatia, a stunning Mediterranean country nestled at the crossroads of Central and Southeast Europe. Renowned for its picturesque coastline, historical cities, and vibrant culture, Croatia has emerged as a popular destination for travelers worldwide. To ensure a smooth and enjoyable travel experience, it is crucial to be well-informed about the visa and travel requirements in Croatia. This comprehensive travel guide provides detailed information on visas, entry regulations, health considerations, and essential tips for a memorable journey.

1. Visa Requirements for Croatia:

1.1 Visa-Free Travel:
Croatia allows visa-free entry for citizens of many countries, making it accessible for tourists from various parts of the globe. Citizens of the European Union (EU) and European Free Trade Association (EFTA) member states can enter Croatia without a visa for an unlimited period. Additionally, citizens from several other countries, including the USA, Canada, Australia, New Zealand, Japan, and many others, can stay in Croatia for up to 90 days within a 180-day period without a visa for tourism purposes.

1.2 Visa on Arrival:
Citizens of some countries that are not eligible for visa-free travel may obtain a visa on arrival. However, it is essential to check the latest information and regulations from official sources before traveling, as visa policies can change.

1.3 Visa Application for Long-term Stay:
For those planning to stay in Croatia for more extended periods, such as for work, study, or family reunification, a visa application needs to be submitted to the Croatian diplomatic mission or consulate in their home country.

2. Passport Requirements:

To enter Croatia, all travelers must possess a valid passport with an expiration date beyond their intended stay. It is advisable to have at least six months' validity remaining on your passport from the date of entry into the country.

3. Travel Insurance:

While not a mandatory requirement for entry, having comprehensive travel insurance is highly recommended. Travel insurance should cover medical emergencies, trip cancellations, baggage loss, and other unforeseen events to provide peace of mind during your trip.

4. Health and Vaccination Requirements:

4.1 Routine Vaccinations:
Before traveling to Croatia, ensure that you are up-to-date with routine vaccinations like measles, mumps, rubella, tetanus, diphtheria, and pertussis.

4.2 COVID-19 Considerations:
Given the ongoing global pandemic, travelers should monitor Croatia's latest COVID-19 regulations, including vaccination requirements, testing protocols, and any quarantine measures in place. It is advisable to check the Croatian government's official website for updated information.

5. *Customs Regulations:*

5.1 Duty-Free Allowance:
Travelers over the age of 18 can import the following duty-free items into Croatia: 200 cigarettes or 100 cigarillos or 50 cigars or 250 grams of smoking tobacco, 1 liter of spirits over 22% alcohol volume or 2 liters of spirits up to 22% alcohol volume, 4 liters of wine, and 16 liters of beer.

5.2 Restricted Items:
Certain items such as firearms, illegal drugs, counterfeit goods, and protected species of plants and animals are strictly prohibited in Croatia.

6. *Currency and Payment:*

6.1 Croatian Kuna (HRK):
The official currency of Croatia is the Croatian Kuna (HRK). While some establishments may accept euros, it is advisable to have some local currency on hand, especially when visiting smaller towns or rural areas.

6.2 Credit Cards and ATMs:
Credit cards are widely accepted in larger cities and tourist areas. ATMs are also readily available, offering a convenient way to withdraw local currency.

7. Language:

The official language of Croatia is Croatian. While English is spoken and understood in tourist areas, learning a few basic Croatian phrases can be appreciated by locals and enhance your travel experience.

8. Transportation:

8.1 Air Travel:
Croatia is well-connected to major international airports, with the busiest being Zagreb International Airport (ZAG), Split Airport (SPU), and Dubrovnik Airport (DBV).

8.2 Public Transportation:

Croatia boasts an efficient and well-developed public transportation system, including buses, trains, and ferries, making it easy to explore the country's diverse regions.

9. Accommodation:

Croatia offers a wide range of accommodation options to suit various budgets and preferences. From luxury hotels to cozy guesthouses and charming boutique properties, travelers can find suitable lodgings across the country.

10. Popular Tourist Destinations:

10.1 Dubrovnik:
Dubrovnik, often referred to as the "Pearl of the Adriatic," is a UNESCO World Heritage site renowned for its ancient walls, Baroque architecture, and breathtaking coastal views.

10.2 Plitvice Lakes National Park:
A natural wonder, Plitvice Lakes National Park boasts a series of cascading lakes and waterfalls, creating a mesmerizing landscape that attracts nature enthusiasts from around the world.

10.3 Split:
Home to the impressive Diocletian's Palace, Split is a vibrant city offering a perfect blend of historical heritage and modern charm.

10.4 Hvar Island:
Famous for its lavender fields and vibrant nightlife, Hvar Island is a favorite destination among young travelers seeking a mix of relaxation and fun.

As you embark on your Croatian adventure, it's essential to be aware of the visa and travel requirements to ensure a smooth journey from start to finish. Croatia's diverse landscapes, rich history, and warm hospitality promise an unforgettable experience for every traveler. By following this comprehensive travel guide, you are well-equipped to make the most of your time in this enchanting Mediterranean gem. So pack your bags, embrace the Croatian spirit, and get ready to create memories that will last a lifetime. Happy travels!

•*Budgeting and Currency*

Welcome to Croatia, a breathtaking country located at the crossroads of Central and Southeast Europe. With its stunning coastline along the Adriatic Sea, rich history, and vibrant culture, Croatia has become an increasingly popular destination for travelers from all around the world. As you plan your trip to this enchanting country, it is essential to have a solid understanding of budgeting and currency matters to ensure a smooth and enjoyable experience. In this comprehensive travel guide, we will delve into the intricacies of budgeting in

Croatia and explore everything you need to know about the local currency and monetary system.

1. *Croatia's Currency and Banking System:*

The official currency of Croatia is the Kuna, abbreviated as HRK. The word "Kuna" actually means "marten," a small mammal whose fur was used as a form of payment in medieval Croatia. The Kuna is further subdivided into 100 Lipa. While Croatia is a part of the European Union, it has not yet adopted the Euro as its official currency. This means that you will need to exchange your money into Kunas upon arrival.

The country has a well-established banking system with numerous ATMs and banks found throughout its major cities and tourist destinations. Major credit and debit cards are widely accepted in hotels, restaurants, and shops, but it is still a good idea to carry some cash for smaller establishments and places that may not accept cards.

2. *Budgeting for Accommodation:*

When it comes to accommodation, Croatia offers a wide range of options to suit every budget. From luxurious hotels to cozy guesthouses and budget-friendly hostels, there is something for everyone.

- Hotels: The cost of hotels in Croatia can vary significantly depending on the location and the level of luxury. In popular tourist destinations like Dubrovnik and Split, expect higher prices during the peak season (summer months). On average, you can find mid-range hotels for around 500 HRK to 800 HRK per night, while luxury hotels can cost upwards of 1000 HRK or more.

- Guesthouses and Apartments: Opting for guesthouses or apartments can be more economical, especially for longer stays or when traveling with a group. Prices for guesthouses can range from 300 HRK to 600 HRK per night, depending on the location and amenities.

- Hostels: Croatia boasts a thriving hostel scene, offering budget-conscious travelers an affordable accommodation option. Dormitory beds in hostels can cost anywhere from 100 HRK to 300 HRK per night.

3. Dining and Food Expenses:

Croatian cuisine is a delightful blend of Mediterranean and Central European flavors, with an emphasis on fresh seafood, grilled meats, olive oil, and aromatic herbs. When it comes to dining, budgeting can be quite flexible, depending on your preferences.

- Restaurants: Dining in restaurants can be reasonably priced, with meals costing between 80 HRK to 150 HRK for a main course. If you want to try local specialties like seafood dishes, expect to pay slightly more.

- Konobas and Local Eateries: For an authentic experience, consider trying out konobas (traditional taverns) and local eateries. Here, you can enjoy hearty meals for around 70 HRK to 120 HRK per dish.

- Street Food and Markets: For a budget-friendly option, explore the street food scene and local markets. Grab a burek (savory pastry) or a delicious seafood snack for as little as 20 HRK to 40 HRK.

4. Transportation Costs:

Getting around Croatia is relatively straightforward, with various transportation options available.

- Public Transport: Cities like Zagreb, Split, and Dubrovnik have well-developed public transportation networks comprising buses and trams. Tickets usually cost around 10 HRK for a single ride, while day passes can range from 30 HRK to 60 HRK, depending on the city.

- Taxis: Taxis are available in most cities, but they tend to be more expensive. Make sure to use licensed taxis and ask for an estimated fare before starting your journey.

- Renting a Car: If you want to explore the country at your own pace, renting a car is an excellent option. Car rental prices can vary from 300 HRK to 600 HRK per day, depending on the type of vehicle and the rental duration.

5. Sightseeing and Activities:

Croatia's natural beauty and historical sites provide a wide array of activities for travelers to enjoy. Here's what you can expect in terms of costs:

- National Parks and Nature Reserves: Entrance fees to national parks like Plitvice Lakes or Krka can range from 100 HRK to 250 HRK, depending on the season and age group.

- Historic Sites and Museums: Admission to historic sites and museums typically costs between 50 HRK to 100 HRK, with discounts available for students and seniors.

- Beaches and Recreational Activities: Many beaches in Croatia are free to access, but some may charge a small fee for amenities like beach chairs and umbrellas. Prices for recreational activities such as water sports and boat tours may vary, so it's best to inquire locally.

6. Shopping and Souvenirs:

Croatia offers a diverse shopping experience, from bustling markets to modern shopping centers. Popular souvenirs include local wines, olive oil, lavender products, and traditional handicrafts.

- Markets and Street Vendors: Haggling is common in markets, so feel free to negotiate for better prices when buying souvenirs. Prices can vary, but you can find unique items for around 50 HRK to 200 HRK.

- Shopping Centers: Prices in shopping centers are generally fixed, and you can find a wide range of goods from clothing to electronics.

As you embark on your journey to Croatia, understanding the country's budgeting and currency system is crucial for a hassle-free experience. With a bit of planning and knowledge, you can make the most of your trip without breaking the bank. From exploring the stunning coastline and indulging in delectable cuisine to immersing yourself in the rich history and culture, Croatia has much to offer every traveler, regardless of their budget. So pack your bags, exchange some Kunas, and get ready for an unforgettable adventure in this charming Balkan gem. Happy travels!

•*Transportation Options*

Croatia, nestled in the heart of Europe, is a captivating country with a rich history, stunning landscapes, and a vibrant culture. From the picturesque Dalmatian coast with its azure waters to the charming medieval towns and lush national parks, Croatia has become an increasingly popular destination for travelers seeking a unique and unforgettable experience. To fully explore this enchanting country, it is essential to understand the various transportation options available. In this comprehensive travel guide, we will delve into the diverse means of transportation in Croatia, including air travel, railways, buses, ferries, and local transportation, highlighting their advantages, drawbacks, and tips for making the most of your journey.

1. Air Travel:

For travelers coming from distant locations, flying into Croatia is the most efficient and time-saving option. The country boasts several international airports, with Zagreb International Airport being the largest and busiest. Other major airports include Split Airport, Dubrovnik Airport, and Zadar Airport. These airports connect Croatia to numerous European cities as well as some destinations outside of Europe.

Advantages:

- Convenient and time-saving for long-distance travelers.
- Wide choice of international flights, especially during peak tourist seasons.
- Efficient connections to major cities and tourist destinations.

Drawbacks:
- Airfare can be expensive, particularly during peak travel periods.
- Limited availability of direct flights to smaller cities and islands.

Tips:
- Book flights well in advance to secure the best deals.
- Consider arriving in one city and departing from another to maximize your itinerary.

2. *Railways:*

Croatia's railway network provides a scenic and leisurely way to explore the country. The railway system connects major cities and towns, offering travelers the opportunity to appreciate the stunning landscapes and picturesque countryside.

Advantages:
- Comfortable and relatively affordable travel.
- Spectacular views during the journey.
- Ideal for shorter distances and city-to-city travel.

Drawbacks:
- Limited coverage to remote regions and islands, where buses and ferries are more prevalent.
- Longer travel times compared to other modes of transportation.

Tips:
- Consider reserving seats on intercity trains during peak tourist seasons to ensure availability.
- Check the schedule in advance, as some routes may have limited daily departures.

3. Buses:

Buses are the backbone of Croatia's transportation system, offering an extensive network that covers almost every corner of the country. They are a popular choice for both locals and tourists due to their affordability and flexibility.

Advantages:
- Comprehensive coverage, including remote regions and islands.
- Frequent departures, especially on popular routes.
- Budget-friendly option for travelers on a tight budget.

Drawbacks:
- Longer travel times compared to flights or private vehicles.
- Limited space for luggage, especially on crowded routes.

Tips:
- Buy tickets at bus stations or online in advance, especially during the peak season.
- Opt for express or premium buses for a more comfortable and faster journey.

4. Ferries:

With its stunning Adriatic coastline and numerous islands, ferries play a crucial role in Croatia's transportation system. They provide a scenic and enjoyable way to travel between the mainland and various islands.

Advantages:
- Spectacular views of the Adriatic Sea and coastal landscapes.
- Direct access to popular islands and coastal destinations.
- Opportunity to experience local island life and culture.

Drawbacks:
- Limited schedules, especially during the offseason.
- May be affected by weather conditions, leading to delays or cancellations.

Tips:
- Check ferry schedules in advance and plan your itinerary accordingly.

- Consider purchasing return tickets if you have fixed travel dates to secure your spot.

5. *Local Transportation:*

Once you arrive at your destination in Croatia, you'll find various options for local transportation within cities and towns. These include buses, trams (in larger cities like Zagreb), taxis, and ride-sharing services.

Advantages:
- Easily accessible and efficient for exploring cities and their attractions.
- Taxis and ride-sharing services offer convenience and flexibility.

Drawbacks:
- Traffic congestion in urban areas, particularly during peak hours.
- Taxi fares may be more expensive, especially for tourists.

Tips:
- In larger cities, use public transportation or ride-sharing services to avoid traffic and parking hassles.
- Negotiate taxi fares in advance or ensure the meter is used.

Croatia's transportation options cater to a diverse range of travelers, ensuring a seamless and memorable journey across this captivating country. Whether you prefer the convenience of air travel, the scenic beauty of trains, the extensive reach of buses, the island-hopping adventure of ferries, or the ease of local transportation, Croatia has it all. To make the most of your trip, plan ahead, consider the pros and cons of each mode of transportation, and embrace the unique experiences that Croatia has to offer. So, pack your bags, embark on an unforgettable adventure, and discover the magic of Croatia through its various transportation options.

CHAPTER THREE

Top Destinations

Zagreb - The Capital City

Welcome to Zagreb, the vibrant and captivating capital city of Croatia. Nestled between the Medvednica Mountains and the Sava River, this charming metropolis offers a perfect blend of old-world charm and modern dynamism. With its rich history, diverse culture, and impressive architecture, Zagreb is a must-visit destination for any traveler exploring Croatia. In this comprehensive travel guide, we will delve into the city's top attractions, cultural experiences, culinary delights, accommodations, and practical travel tips, ensuring you make the most of your visit to this gem of Eastern Europe.

I. History and Culture:

1. Historical Overview:
Zagreb boasts a fascinating history dating back to Roman times. It officially became the capital of Croatia in 1557, and through the centuries, it evolved into a significant cultural and economic hub. The city's architecture showcases influences

from various periods, with the Upper Town featuring well-preserved medieval structures and the Lower Town displaying a blend of neoclassical and art nouveau styles.

2. Exploring the Old Town:
Begin your Zagreb adventure in the Upper Town (Gornji Grad), the oldest part of the city. Here, you'll find iconic landmarks like St. Mark's Church, with its beautifully tiled roof, and the Lotrščak Tower, which offers panoramic views of the city. Don't miss the Zagreb Cathedral and the Stone Gate, both of which hold great religious and historical significance.

3. Museums and Galleries:
Zagreb is a treasure trove of museums and galleries. The Croatian Museum of Naïve Art, the Museum of Broken Relationships, and the Archaeological Museum are just a few of the institutions that offer unique insights into the country's art, culture, and history.

II. Cultural Experiences:

1. Festivals and Events:
Immerse yourself in the vibrant culture of Zagreb by attending one of its numerous festivals and events. The Advent in Zagreb is particularly special, transforming the city into a winter wonderland with dazzling lights, Christmas markets, and a delightful atmosphere.

2. Mirogoj Cemetery:
While it may sound unconventional, a visit to the Mirogoj Cemetery is a poignant cultural experience. This stunning cemetery is an architectural masterpiece and a final resting place for many prominent Croatians.

3. Performing Arts:
Zagreb has a thriving performing arts scene, with its National Theatre and Croatian National Opera and Ballet staging world-class performances throughout the year. Catch a show to appreciate the city's artistic prowess.

III. Culinary Delights:

1. Traditional Cuisine:
No travel guide to Zagreb would be complete without mentioning its delectable cuisine. Sample traditional dishes like štrukli (a cheese-filled pastry), kulen (spicy sausage), and pašticada (beef stew) to experience the authentic flavors of Croatia.

2. Dolac Market:
Visit the bustling Dolac Market, where locals and tourists alike gather to purchase fresh produce, cheeses, meats, and handmade crafts. It's a fantastic place to get a taste of local life and pick up some souvenirs.

IV. Accommodations:

1. Luxury Hotels:
Zagreb offers a range of luxury hotels that provide top-notch amenities and services. From historic properties in the heart of the city to modern five-star establishments, you'll find plenty of options to suit your preferences.

2. Boutique Stays:
For a more intimate experience, consider staying at one of Zagreb's boutique hotels or guesthouses. These charming accommodations often reflect the city's unique character and provide personalized attention to guests.

V. Practical Travel Tips:

1. Best Time to Visit:
The ideal time to visit Zagreb is during the shoulder seasons of spring and autumn when the weather is pleasant, and tourist crowds are thinner. If you're a fan of winter festivities, consider visiting during Advent.

2. Getting Around:
Zagreb's public transportation system is efficient and cost-effective. Trams and buses connect various parts of the city, making it easy to navigate the sights.

3. Safety and Culture:

Zagreb is generally a safe city for travelers, but it's always wise to exercise caution and be mindful of your belongings. Familiarize yourself with the local customs and etiquette to show respect to the residents.

Zagreb, the enchanting capital city of Croatia, is a destination that captivates the hearts of all who visit. With its historical landmarks, vibrant cultural scene, delectable cuisine, and welcoming accommodations, Zagreb has something to offer every traveler. Whether you're interested in exploring its rich history, indulging in local delicacies, or simply soaking in the city's charm, Zagreb promises an unforgettable experience. So pack your bags, embrace the allure of this hidden gem, and prepare to create memories that will last a lifetime in the heart of Croatia.

Must-Visit Attractions

Welcome to the vibrant capital city of Croatia – Zagreb! Nestled between the Sava River and the southern slopes of Mount Medvednica, Zagreb offers a unique blend of historical charm, cultural treasures, and modern attractions. This bustling metropolis is a haven for travelers seeking a memorable European experience. In this comprehensive travel guide, we will explore the must-visit attractions that make Zagreb an enchanting destination worth exploring. From historic landmarks and museums to picturesque parks and lively markets, there's something for every type of traveler in this charming city.

I. Historical and Architectural Gems:

1. Zagreb Cathedral (Cathedral of the Assumption of the Blessed Virgin Mary):
The Zagreb Cathedral, also known as the Cathedral of St. Stephen, is a masterpiece of Gothic architecture and a symbol of the city. Its twin spires dominate the skyline, and the interior is adorned with impressive frescoes and religious artifacts. Don't miss the chance to climb the bell tower for breathtaking views of the city.

2. St. Mark's Church (Crkva sv. Marka):
Located in the Upper Town, St. Mark's Church is one of the most recognizable landmarks in Zagreb. Its distinctive roof features the medieval coat of arms of Croatia, Dalmatia, and Slavonia on one side, and the emblem of Zagreb on the other. The church's interior boasts beautiful Baroque altars and Gothic sculptures.

3. Ban Jelačić Square (Trg bana Jelačića):
Named after the beloved 19th-century governor, Ban Josip Jelačić, this lively square is the heart of Zagreb's social and cultural life. Surrounded by historic buildings, shops, and restaurants, it's an excellent starting point for exploring the city's attractions.

4. Dolac Market:
For a genuine local experience, visit Dolac Market, Zagreb's most famous open-air market. Here, you'll find an array of fresh produce, local delicacies, traditional crafts, and souvenirs. Engage with the friendly vendors and immerse yourself in the city's vibrant atmosphere.

II. Cultural and Artistic Treasures:

1. Croatian National Theatre (Hrvatsko narodno kazalište):
The Croatian National Theatre is a grand neo-baroque building that hosts opera, ballet, and drama performances. If you're a fan of the arts, be sure to catch a show to experience the city's cultural richness.

2. Mimara Museum:
Housing an extensive collection of art and historical artifacts, the Mimara Museum is a must-visit for art enthusiasts. From Egyptian antiquities to European paintings, the museum offers a captivating journey through various periods and civilizations.

3. Museum of Broken Relationships:
This one-of-a-kind museum showcases personal items from failed relationships, each with its own emotional story attached. It's a moving and thought-provoking experience that has touched the hearts of visitors from around the world.

4. Croatian Museum of Naïve Art:
Discover the charm of naïve art at this museum, which houses an impressive collection of artworks by self-taught artists. The colorful and imaginative pieces provide insight into the untrained artists' unique perspectives.

III. Green Oases and Parks:

1. Maksimir Park:
Escape the urban hustle and bustle by heading to Maksimir Park, one of the oldest public parks in Europe. The park features beautiful lakes, walking trails, and a zoo, making it a perfect spot for a leisurely afternoon.

2. Jarun Lake:
For a taste of the local's outdoor lifestyle, visit Jarun Lake. This artificial lake offers various recreational activities, including swimming, sailing, and cycling. There are also numerous cafes and bars along the lake, where you can relax and enjoy the views.

3. Bundek Park:
Located near the city center, Bundek Park is a serene and picturesque park with a large lake. It's an ideal spot for a relaxing picnic or a peaceful stroll amid nature.

IV. Unique Experiences:

1. Zagreb 360°:
For panoramic views of the city, head to Zagreb 360°, an observation deck located on the 16th floor of the Zagreb Eye Skyscraper. Take in the breathtaking vistas, day or night, and see the city from a whole new perspective.

2. Advent in Zagreb:
If you visit Zagreb during the holiday season, be sure to experience the city's magical Advent festivities. Zagreb has been voted the best Christmas market in Europe multiple times, and it comes alive with enchanting lights, festive stalls, and joyful celebrations.

3. Medvednica Mountain:
Nature lovers and outdoor enthusiasts shouldn't miss the chance to explore Medvednica Mountain, which offers hiking trails, stunning viewpoints, and opportunities for adventure and relaxation in the great outdoors.

As our comprehensive travel guide comes to an end, we hope you're inspired to embark on a journey to Zagreb, Croatia's enchanting capital city. From historical landmarks and architectural marvels to cultural treasures and natural beauty, Zagreb offers a diverse range of attractions that cater to every traveler's interests. Immerse yourself in the city's rich history, explore its vibrant culture, and enjoy the warm hospitality of the locals. Zagreb is a destination that will leave a lasting impression and create unforgettable memories for every visitor. So pack your bags, and get ready to experience the magic of Zagreb!

Dining and Nightlife

Zagreb, the capital city of Croatia, is a vibrant metropolis that offers a rich blend of history, culture, and gastronomy. In this comprehensive travel guide, we will delve into the dining and nightlife scene in Zagreb, showcasing the city's culinary delights and buzzing after-dark activities. From traditional Croatian cuisine to contemporary fusion restaurants, and from lively bars to stylish nightclubs, Zagreb has something to offer every palate and preference. Join us on a gastronomic and nocturnal journey through Zagreb's best dining and nightlife venues.

1. Traditional Croatian Cuisine

Zagreb is a city that takes pride in its culinary heritage, offering visitors a chance to savor authentic Croatian dishes. Traditional cuisine is characterized by hearty, flavorful meals that showcase the country's diverse regional influences. One cannot miss trying some of the following dishes:

a. Štrukli: A must-try dish, Štrukli is a type of pastry filled with cottage cheese or various sweet or savory fillings. It's a favorite among locals and is served in many restaurants across the city.

b. Peka: Peka is a traditional Croatian way of slow-cooking meat and vegetables, typically lamb or octopus, under a bell-like dome. The result is tender, flavorful, and aromatic.

c. Black Risotto: Known as "Crni Rižot" in Croatian, this unique dish is made with cuttlefish or squid ink, giving it its distinctive color and a rich seafood taste.

d. Ćevapi: Originally from the Balkans, these small, grilled sausages made from minced meat (usually a mix of beef, lamb, and pork) are served in a flatbread with chopped onions and a red pepper-based sauce.

2. Restaurants and Gastronomic Experiences

Zagreb boasts a diverse culinary scene, ranging from traditional taverns to innovative fine-dining restaurants. Here are some noteworthy establishments:

a. Vinodol: Located in the heart of the city, Vinodol offers a blend of traditional Croatian dishes with a modern twist. The restaurant's elegant ambiance and extensive wine list make it a favorite among locals and tourists alike.

b. Agava: Situated in a charming courtyard, Agava impresses with its Mediterranean-inspired menu and delightful terrace seating. The restaurant often hosts live music, adding to the overall dining experience.

c. Takenoko: For those craving something different, Takenoko serves up delicious Japanese cuisine, including sushi, sashimi, and traditional teppanyaki dishes.

d. Mundoaka Street Food: This vibrant eatery focuses on fusion street food, combining Croatian ingredients with international flavors. It's the perfect spot for a quick, satisfying bite.

3. Cafés and Coffee Culture

Croatians have a strong coffee culture, and Zagreb is no exception. The city is dotted with charming cafés where locals enjoy their daily cup of coffee and engage in leisurely conversations. Some notable cafés include:

a. Velvet Café: Known for its cozy atmosphere and unique décor, Velvet Café is a great place to relax and enjoy a cup of expertly brewed coffee.

b. Johann Franck: Established in 1827, this iconic café has been a meeting place for generations of locals. It's an excellent spot for people-watching and trying traditional Croatian desserts.

c. Eli's Caffe: Situated in the heart of the city, Eli's Caffe is a popular spot among the younger crowd. The café serves a wide range of coffee specialties and has a lively ambiance.

4. *Nightlife and Bars*

As the sun sets, Zagreb's nightlife comes alive with a diverse range of bars and pubs catering to various tastes. Whether you prefer a casual pub, a stylish cocktail bar, or a live music venue, Zagreb has it all:

a. Tkalciceva Street: This bustling street is a hub for nightlife, lined with bars, pubs, and restaurants. It's an excellent place for bar-hopping and experiencing the city's vibrant atmosphere.

b. Hemingway Bar: If you're a cocktail enthusiast, Hemingway Bar is a must-visit. This stylish bar is known for its creative cocktails and a wide selection of premium spirits.

c. Boogaloo: For fans of live music and dancing, Boogaloo is a popular choice. This nightclub hosts various events and concerts, covering a wide range of musical genres.

d. Swanky Monkey Garden: Located in the heart of Zagreb, this hip bar offers a unique outdoor setting, making it an ideal spot for warm summer evenings.

5. Nightclubs and Entertainment Venues

Zagreb's nightlife wouldn't be complete without its lively nightclubs and entertainment venues. From electronic dance music to live bands, there's something for everyone:

a. Revelin: Situated within the city's historic walls, Revelin is a premier nightclub known for its energetic atmosphere and top-notch DJs.

b. Tvornica Kulture: A former industrial complex transformed into a concert venue, Tvornica Kulture hosts various events, including concerts, DJ performances, and cultural gatherings.

c. Opera Club: For those who prefer a more sophisticated setting, Opera Club offers a mix of electronic and house music in a stylish, opera-themed environment.

Zagreb's dining and nightlife scene are integral parts of the city's identity, providing visitors with a taste of Croatia's rich culinary heritage and an opportunity to experience its vibrant after-dark culture. From traditional Croatian dishes to international cuisines, and from cozy cafés to lively nightclubs, Zagreb has something for every traveler seeking an unforgettable gastronomic and nocturnal journey. So, immerse yourself in the local flavors, enjoy the buzzing nightlife, and create memories that will last a lifetime in Croatia's captivating capital.

• *Dubrovnik - The Pearl of the Adriatic*

Nestled along the shimmering waters of the Adriatic Sea, Dubrovnik stands proudly as a timeless jewel on the southern coast of Croatia. Often referred to as "The Pearl of the Adriatic," this ancient city has captivated travelers for centuries with its stunning architecture, rich history, and breathtaking natural beauty. From its imposing medieval walls to its picturesque coastline, Dubrovnik offers a myriad of experiences that cater to all types of travelers. In this comprehensive Croatia travel guide, we will delve into the enchanting city of Dubrovnik, exploring its history, culture, top attractions, cuisine, and practical travel tips, providing you with all the information you need to embark on an unforgettable journey to this magnificent destination.

1. *Historical Background:*

Dubrovnik's history can be traced back to the 7th century when it was founded as a Byzantine stronghold. Over the centuries, the city grew into a prosperous maritime republic, establishing itself as a prominent player in trade and diplomacy in the Mediterranean. Its strategic location along major trade routes contributed to its wealth and cultural exchange. However, the rise of powerful neighboring empires, including the Ottoman Empire and Venice, challenged Dubrovnik's independence and led to periods of conquest and decline.

Despite these challenges, Dubrovnik managed to preserve its autonomy and unique identity through diplomacy and strategic alliances. In the 15th and 16th centuries, the city flourished as a center of art and culture, leaving behind an impressive architectural legacy that continues to enthrall visitors today. In 1979, UNESCO recognized the Old City of Dubrovnik as a World Heritage Site, acknowledging its exceptional historical significance and well-preserved medieval architecture.

2. Top Attractions:

a. The Old City Walls: The iconic medieval walls, dating back to the 10th century, are undoubtedly Dubrovnik's most famous attraction. Extending almost 2 kilometers around the Old City, these sturdy fortifications offer panoramic views of the Adriatic Sea, red-tiled roofs, and narrow cobblestone streets.

b. Stradun (Placa): The main street of the Old City, Stradun, is the bustling heart of Dubrovnik. Lined with elegant Baroque buildings, shops, and restaurants, it is the perfect place to soak in the city's vibrant atmosphere.

c. Dubrovnik Cathedral: Also known as the Cathedral of the Assumption, this stunning Baroque-style cathedral houses an impressive treasury and artworks by renowned artists such as Titian and Rafael.

d. Rector's Palace: A magnificent blend of Gothic, Renaissance, and Baroque architecture, the Rector's Palace showcases Dubrovnik's historical grandeur. Today, it houses the Cultural Historical Museum.

e. Lokrum Island: Just a short boat ride from Dubrovnik, Lokrum Island offers a serene escape with beautiful gardens, peacocks, and pristine beaches. Legend has it that Richard the Lionheart was shipwrecked here.

f. Mount Srđ: For panoramic views of Dubrovnik and its surroundings, take a cable car ride to the top of Mount Srđ. On clear days, you can see the Elaphiti Islands in the distance.

3. *Cultural Delights:*

Dubrovnik's culture is a harmonious blend of its medieval past and modern influences. The city hosts numerous festivals and events throughout the year, celebrating everything from music and art to theater and film. The Dubrovnik Summer Festival, held annually from July to August, is one of the most prominent cultural events, featuring a wide array of performances in the open-air venues of the Old City.

Additionally, Dubrovnik's art scene flourishes with local galleries showcasing contemporary Croatian artists, as well as traditional crafts like embroidery and pottery. Visitors can immerse themselves in the local culture by attending folk dance performances, sampling regional cuisine, and engaging with the warm and welcoming locals.

4. Gastronomy:

Croatian cuisine is a delightful fusion of Mediterranean and Balkan flavors, and Dubrovnik offers a tantalizing variety of dishes to please any palate. Seafood is a highlight in the city's culinary repertoire, with dishes like black risotto (made with cuttlefish ink) and grilled Adriatic fish being must-tries. You can also savor traditional meat-based dishes like peka, a slow-cooked mix of meat, potatoes, and vegetables baked in a covered dish.

To complement your meal, indulge in local wines, particularly those produced in the nearby Pelješac Peninsula and Konavle region. Croatia's wine culture dates back to ancient times, and today, it boasts an impressive selection of reds and whites.

5. Practical Travel Tips:

a. Best Time to Visit: The peak tourist season in Dubrovnik runs from June to August when the weather is warm and ideal for beach activities. However, for a more relaxed experience and pleasant weather, consider visiting in the shoulder seasons of spring (April to May) and autumn (September to October).

b. Currency: Croatia's currency is the kuna (HRK). While some establishments may accept euros, it's best to have kunas for smoother transactions.

c. Language: Croatian is the official language, but English is widely spoken in tourist areas.

d. Transportation: Dubrovnik is well-connected by air, with Dubrovnik Airport catering to both domestic and international flights. Public buses and taxis are available for local transportation, but walking is the best way to explore the compact Old City.

e. Accommodation: Dubrovnik offers a range of accommodations, from luxury hotels to budget-friendly hostels. Staying within the city walls provides a unique experience, but there are also excellent options outside the Old City.

f. Respect Local Customs: Dubrovnik is a conservative city, so it's essential to dress modestly when visiting religious sites or public places.

Dubrovnik, the Pearl of the Adriatic, is a destination that leaves an indelible mark on all who have the privilege of experiencing its beauty. From its ancient walls and historical landmarks to its vibrant culture and delectable cuisine, Dubrovnik presents a captivating blend of the old and the new. As you wander through its narrow streets and soak in the breathtaking views of the Adriatic, you'll be transported to a bygone era while cherishing every moment of your contemporary adventure. With this Croatia travel guide as your companion, embark on a journey of a lifetime to Dubrovnik and create memories that will stay with you forever.

Exploring the Old Town

Croatia is a country renowned for its stunning landscapes, azure waters, and rich history. Among its many gems, Dubrovnik stands out as a true gem on the Adriatic coast. With its picturesque location and well-preserved medieval architecture, the Old Town of Dubrovnik is a captivating destination that takes visitors on a timeless journey through history.

In this Croatia travel guide, we will delve into the wonders of exploring the Old Town of Dubrovnik, where the past comes alive and the present is filled with an array of cultural delights. From the fortified walls to the charming narrow streets, this ancient city invites travelers to immerse themselves in its beauty, history, and unique experiences.

1. Historical Background
The history of Dubrovnik dates back to the 7th century when it was established as a Byzantine stronghold. Over the centuries, it flourished as an independent maritime republic, becoming a powerful trade center and establishing its sovereignty. The Old Town, also known as the "Pearl of the Adriatic," grew and evolved within fortified walls, which were constructed during the 12th to 17th centuries to protect the city from invaders. The Old Town's strategic location made it a significant player in regional politics and commerce during the medieval period, fostering a prosperous and culturally rich society.

2. Entering the Gates of the Old Town

As travelers approach the Old Town, they are greeted by the imposing Pile Gate, one of the main entrances. Passing through this gate, visitors are immediately transported into a different era. The smooth, polished limestone streets, polished by centuries of footsteps, lead the way through a maze of history and charm. The gate is guarded by the statue of St. Blaise, the patron saint of Dubrovnik, an iconic symbol of protection for the city.

3. Stradun - The Main Street

Stradun, also known as Placa, is the main thoroughfare that cuts through the heart of the Old Town. This limestone-paved street is flanked by elegant Renaissance and Baroque buildings, housing cafes, shops, and historical landmarks. Take a leisurely stroll down Stradun, observing the architectural marvels and savoring the charming atmosphere. At night, the street is illuminated, creating a magical ambiance perfect for evening strolls.

4. Dubrovnik's Architectural Gems

The Old Town is a treasure trove of architectural wonders. The Franciscan Monastery is one such gem, featuring a beautiful Romanesque-Gothic cloister and Europe's third oldest pharmacy, which has been operating since the 14th century. The Rector's Palace, a masterpiece of Gothic-Renaissance architecture, is another must-visit site that once served as the seat of the Dubrovnik Republic's government. Today, it houses the Cultural Historical Museum, offering insight into the city's political and cultural heritage.

5. Dubrovnik Cathedral

The Dubrovnik Cathedral, also known as the Assumption Cathedral, is a magnificent Baroque structure dedicated to the Assumption of the Virgin Mary. The cathedral's facade is adorned with sculptures, and its interior houses an impressive treasury of religious relics and artworks.

6. City Walls of Dubrovnik

One of the most iconic features of Dubrovnik is its imposing city walls. These well-preserved defensive walls encompass the entire Old Town and provide panoramic views of the city and the Adriatic Sea. Walking along the walls offers an unparalleled experience, providing glimpses into the past and present of this historic city. The walls were essential for protecting Dubrovnik from invasions, and they continue to guard its beauty to this day.

7. Fortresses and Bastions

The city walls are fortified with several forts and bastions that were strategically placed to safeguard the city. The most prominent of these is the Lovrijenac Fortress, also known as "Dubrovnik's Gibraltar." Standing on a rocky cliff outside the western wall, Lovrijenac played a crucial role in defending the city from attackers. Today, it hosts theatrical performances and concerts during the Dubrovnik Summer Festival, adding a cultural touch to its historical significance.

8. Onofrio's Fountain

Onofrio's Fountain, located near the Pile Gate, is an elegant circular fountain built in 1438. It was a vital source of freshwater for the residents of Dubrovnik, supplied through an aqueduct system that originated from a spring 12 kilometers away. The fountain's beautiful design and functional significance make it a favorite gathering spot for both locals and tourists.

9. Dubrovnik's Culture and Festivals

Dubrovnik has a vibrant cultural scene, and visiting during one of its festivals can be a memorable experience. The Dubrovnik Summer Festival is the highlight of the city's cultural calendar, featuring a diverse program of theater, music, dance, and art. Held from July to August, this festival celebrates Croatia's cultural heritage and attracts performers and visitors from around the world.

10. Island-Hopping from Dubrovnik

Apart from the enchanting Old Town, Dubrovnik also serves as a gateway to numerous nearby islands. Take a day trip to the nearby Elafiti Islands, a small archipelago boasting natural beauty, tranquil beaches, and charming villages. The island of Lokrum, just a short boat ride away, offers lush botanical gardens, historical ruins, and a salt lake ideal for swimming.

11. Culinary Delights

No travel guide to Dubrovnik would be complete without mentioning its delightful cuisine. Seafood reigns supreme here, and you'll find a plethora of restaurants offering fresh catches from the Adriatic Sea. Try the local specialty, "black risotto," made with cuttlefish ink, or indulge in a hearty dish of "Pasticada," a slow-cooked beef stew with a unique blend of flavors. Pair your meals with local wines, such as Plavac Mali or Dingač, for an authentic culinary experience.

Exploring the Old Town of Dubrovnik in Croatia is a journey that transports visitors to a world of historical splendor, cultural richness, and captivating beauty. From the ancient city walls to the charming cobblestone streets, every corner of the Old Town exudes an unmistakable charm. As you wander through its alleys, admire its architectural marvels, and take in the breathtaking vistas, you'll discover why Dubrovnik is rightfully considered one of the most enchanting cities on the Adriatic coast. Whether you are a history enthusiast, a culture seeker, or simply a lover of natural beauty, Dubrovnik promises an unforgettable experience that will leave a lasting imprint on your heart and soul.

Game of Thrones Filming Locations

Dubrovnik, Croatia, is a city of stunning beauty that has captured the hearts of travelers from all over the world. While it boasts a rich history and architectural wonders, it has also become famous for being one of the primary filming locations for the acclaimed television series "Game of Thrones." This fantasy epic, based on the novels by George R.R. Martin, has brought worldwide attention to Dubrovnik, attracting legions of fans eager to immerse themselves in the real-life settings of Westeros and Essos. In this travel guide, we'll embark on an extraordinary journey to explore the enchanting Game of Thrones filming locations in Dubrovnik, delving into the rich history and culture of this remarkable Croatian city.

1. Dubrovnik: The Pearl of the Adriatic

Before we delve into the Game of Thrones filming locations, it's essential to understand the allure of Dubrovnik itself. Often referred to as the "Pearl of the Adriatic," Dubrovnik boasts a UNESCO World Heritage-listed Old Town filled with ancient walls, charming cobblestone streets, majestic churches, and historic palaces. The city's stunning location on the Adriatic coast adds to its charm, making it an ideal destination for travelers seeking a mix of history, culture, and breathtaking scenery.

2. Dubrovnik's Role in Game of Thrones

The producers of "Game of Thrones" recognized the inherent beauty and grandeur of Dubrovnik, making it a prime choice for several key filming locations. Dubrovnik stands in for the capital city of Westeros, King's Landing, known for its political intrigue, power struggles, and dramatic events that unfold throughout the series. Its unique architecture and coastal setting lent themselves perfectly to creating the iconic city portrayed in the show.

3. Exploring the Game of Thrones Filming Locations:

3.1 Pile Gate and Dubrovnik City Walls

The journey to the Game of Thrones filming locations begins at Pile Gate, the main entrance to Dubrovnik's Old Town. Pile Gate was used in various scenes, including the memorable moment when King Joffrey faced a riot and was pelted with insults and filth. From here, visitors can ascend the ancient city walls, which offer unparalleled views of the terracotta-roofed buildings and the sparkling Adriatic Sea. The walls feature prominently in many scenes, most notably the iconic walk of shame endured by Cersei Lannister.

3.2 Fort Lovrijenac (Red Keep)

Perched dramatically atop a cliff, Fort Lovrijenac, also known as the "Red Keep" in the show, overlooks the sea and the city. This formidable fortress played a crucial role in the series as the seat of power for the rulers of King's Landing. Many pivotal scenes featuring the Lannisters and other noble houses were filmed within its walls, making it an essential stop for any Game of Thrones fan.

3.3 Trsteno Arboretum (King's Landing Gardens)

A short journey from Dubrovnik leads to the Trsteno Arboretum, a lush garden estate filled with centuries-old trees, fountains, and exotic plants. This enchanting location served as the gardens of King's Landing, where memorable conversations between characters took place, most notably those involving the cunning Queen of Thorns, Lady Olenna Tyrell.

3.4 Lokrum Island (Qarth)

Just a 15-minute boat ride from Dubrovnik, Lokrum Island is a paradise of botanical gardens and pristine beaches. In "Game of Thrones," it was transformed into the city of Qarth, where Daenerys Targaryen sought support for her journey to reclaim the Iron Throne. The island's picturesque landscapes and the medieval Benedictine monastery further add to its allure.

3.5 Dubac Quarry (Dragonpit)

The Dubac Quarry is a disused limestone quarry located near Dubrovnik, which was used as the setting for the Dragonpit in the show's seventh season. The Dragonpit, an ancient colosseum-like structure, plays a pivotal role in the series' climax, where characters meet to discuss the looming threat of the White Walkers. Today, the quarry remains an awe-inspiring site to visit, offering panoramic views of the city and the sea.

4. *Embracing Dubrovnik's Culture and Cuisine:*

Apart from the Game of Thrones filming locations, Dubrovnik has much more to offer. Travelers can explore the city's rich cultural heritage by visiting museums, art galleries, and attending traditional music and dance performances. Additionally, sampling local cuisine is a must-do experience, with fresh seafood, olive oil, and Mediterranean flavors dominating the menus of the city's restaurants and taverns.

5. *Practical Tips for Game of Thrones Fans:*

To make the most of a Game of Thrones-themed trip to Dubrovnik, it's essential to plan ahead. This section of the guide provides practical tips on the best time to visit, accommodations, transportation options, and guided tours that focus on the show's filming locations.

Dubrovnik, Croatia, is a destination that effortlessly weaves together history, natural beauty, and the magical allure of a fantasy world. For Game of Thrones fans and travelers alike, exploring the filming locations in Dubrovnik is an experience like no other. From the mighty city walls to the enchanting gardens, every corner of this captivating city holds a piece of the Westerosi legacy. As you wander through the streets that once echoed with the clashing of swords and the whispering of intrigues, you'll not only discover the allure of this fictional world but also immerse yourself in the timeless charm of Dubrovnik, the Pearl of the Adriatic.

•*Split - Ancient History and Modern Vibes*

Nestled on the eastern shores of the Adriatic Sea, Croatia is a country renowned for its stunning coastline, rich history, and vibrant culture. Among its many gems, Split stands out as a captivating city that seamlessly blends ancient history with modern vibes. This Croatia travel guide will take you on a journey through the ages, exploring the fascinating historical sites and the dynamic contemporary scene of Split.

I. Historical Background

1. Early Settlements and Roman Heritage
Split's history dates back over 1,700 years when the Roman Emperor Diocletian chose this location to build his grand palace. The Diocletian's Palace, a UNESCO World Heritage site, remains the heart and soul of Split, offering a glimpse into the opulent life of the Roman era. Visitors can explore the Peristyle, the impressive central square of the palace, and the underground cellars that once served as storage and shelter.

2. Medieval Influence and Venetian Era
Following the decline of the Roman Empire, Split experienced various rule changes and influences. During the medieval period, it was ruled by the Croatian kings and Hungarian monarchs. Later, it came under the Venetian Republic's control, leaving behind an architectural legacy that can be admired in many of the city's palaces and buildings.

3. Ottoman and Austro-Hungarian Influence
The Ottoman Empire briefly had an impact on the region in the 16th century, but it was the Austro-Hungarian Empire that significantly shaped Split's urban development during the 19th and early 20th centuries. The architecture of the time, characterized by neoclassical and Secessionist styles, still adorns the city's streets, adding to its unique charm.

II. Exploring Ancient Treasures

1. Diocletian's Palace and Peristyle

As the most iconic attraction in Split, the Diocletian's Palace is a must-visit for history enthusiasts. Stroll through the Peristyle, flanked by ancient columns and featuring the imposing Sphinx statues, and marvel at the Cathedral of Saint Domnius, one of the world's oldest cathedrals, which was originally Diocletian's mausoleum.

2. Cathedral of Saint Domnius

The Cathedral's bell tower offers a magnificent panorama of Split's old town and the surrounding Adriatic coastline. Inside, visitors can explore the crypt, treasury, and climb to the top of the bell tower for breathtaking views.

3. Temple of Jupiter

Located within the Diocletian's Palace, the Temple of Jupiter is a fascinating historical site. The temple's central position and unique architectural features make it a captivating spot to explore.

4. Split City Museum and Archaeological Museum

For a deeper understanding of Split's history, a visit to the Split City Museum and Archaeological Museum is highly recommended. These museums house an impressive collection of artifacts, including ancient Roman sculptures, medieval artifacts, and archaeological finds from various periods.

III. *Enchanting Modern Vibes*

1. Riva Promenade
The Riva promenade is the heart of Split's modern life, a vibrant waterfront promenade lined with cafes, restaurants, and palm trees. Enjoy a leisurely stroll, savor local delicacies, and soak in the atmosphere of this bustling area.

2. Marjan Hill
Escape the urban bustle by hiking up Marjan Hill, a lush green oasis that offers fantastic views of the city and the surrounding islands. The hill is also dotted with hermitages, churches, and hiking trails, making it an ideal spot for nature lovers and outdoor enthusiasts.

3. Bačvice Beach
Croatia's coastline is renowned for its beautiful beaches, and Bačvice is Split's most famous sandy beach. Join the locals in a game of picigin, a traditional ball game played in shallow waters, or simply relax and bask in the sun.

4. Trg Republike (Republic Square)
Located in the heart of Split, Trg Republike is a lively square surrounded by historical buildings and modern cafes. It's an excellent place to sit back and

people-watch, as well as to witness cultural events and performances.

IV. Cultural Delights and Gastronomy

1. Croatian National Theatre Split
Art and culture thrive in Split, and a visit to the Croatian National Theatre is a fantastic way to experience the city's vibrant arts scene. Enjoy ballet, opera, and theatrical performances in a stunning historical venue.

2. Pazar Market
To get a taste of authentic local life and gastronomy, head to the Pazar Market. Here, you can find an array of fresh produce, local delicacies, and handmade crafts. It's an ideal place to try traditional Dalmatian dishes and mingle with friendly locals.

3. Wine and Dine
Croatian cuisine is a delightful blend of Mediterranean and continental influences. Don't miss the chance to savor fresh seafood, olive oil, prosciutto, and local wines. Many restaurants in Split offer outdoor seating, providing a charming ambiance as you indulge in the flavors of the region.

V. Island Hopping and Beyond

1. Hvar Island

Embrace the adventure of island hopping from Split, with Hvar Island being a popular choice. Known for its lavender fields, crystal-clear waters, and lively nightlife, Hvar is a paradise for nature enthusiasts and party-goers alike.

2. Brač Island
Another gem to explore is Brač Island, famous for its stunning Zlatni Rat (Golden Horn) beach, which shifts its shape with the changing currents and winds. The island is also known for its exquisite stone, which has been used in the construction of famous buildings worldwide.

Split offers a captivating blend of ancient history and modern vibrancy, making it an ideal destination for travelers seeking a unique experience. From exploring ancient Roman heritage in the Diocletian's Palace to immersing oneself in the lively atmosphere of Riva promenade, Split captivates visitors with its rich history, cultural delights, and breathtaking scenery. Whether you're a history buff, an outdoor enthusiast, or a foodie looking to savor authentic Dalmatian flavors, Split has something to offer everyone, leaving a lasting impression that will beckon you back time and time again.

Diocletian's Palace

Nestled along the shimmering Adriatic coast, Croatia has become an increasingly popular travel destination, attracting millions of tourists every year. One of its crown jewels is the ancient city of Split, which is home to the remarkable Diocletian's Palace. Steeped in history, culture, and architectural grandeur, this UNESCO World Heritage site offers visitors an unforgettable journey back in time. In this Croatia travel guide, we'll explore the captivating allure of Diocletian's Palace, uncovering its rich past, architectural marvels, and the myriad experiences that await travelers in this enchanting corner of the world.

1. *Historical Background:*

Diocletian's Palace, located in the heart of Split, was built by the Roman emperor Diocletian at the turn of the 4th century AD. Diocletian was one of the most influential and powerful emperors in Roman history, known for his stern rule and persecutions against Christians. After reigning for more than two decades, he decided to retire and chose the site of present-day Split to build his grand retirement palace.

Construction of the palace began in AD 295 and took around a decade to complete. The palace was intended to be a lavish residence for the retired emperor, complete with luxurious living quarters, temples, administrative buildings, and even a private mausoleum.

2. Architectural Marvels:

Diocletian's Palace is an architectural masterpiece, blending elements of classical Roman, Greek, and even Egyptian styles. The sprawling complex spans approximately 7 acres and is surrounded by imposing walls and fortified gates. The palace's layout follows a well-organized grid pattern, with two main streets crossing each other at right angles, dividing the palace into four quarters.

A. Peristyle Square:
The heart of Diocletian's Palace is the Peristyle Square, an open courtyard flanked by impressive columns and adorned with exquisite statues. This area served as the ceremonial center of the palace, where important events and gatherings took place.

B. Diocletian's Mausoleum (Cathedral of Saint Domnius):
One of the most iconic structures within the palace is the Mausoleum of Diocletian, which later became the Cathedral of Saint Domnius. This cylindrical building is a fine example of ancient Roman architecture and is dedicated to the patron saint of Split, Saint Domnius. The cathedral's bell tower offers a breathtaking view of the city and the Adriatic Sea.

C. Vestibule:

Adjacent to the Peristyle Square is the Vestibule, an awe-inspiring domed chamber that served as the entrance hall to the emperor's private apartments. The Vestibule's perfect symmetry and intricate decorations make it a sight to behold.

D. Basement Halls:
Below the palace lies an intricate network of underground halls and passageways. These substructures served various functions, including storage, living quarters for servants, and likely also housed the palace's heating system. Today, the basement halls are open to visitors and offer a fascinating glimpse into the engineering prowess of the ancient Romans.

3. Modern-Day Attractions:

Beyond its historical significance, Diocletian's Palace is a vibrant hub of modern-day activities, ensuring that visitors are never short of things to do and experience.

A. Shopping and Dining:
The charming streets within the palace walls are lined with shops, boutiques, and restaurants. Tourists can indulge in local delicacies, sample Dalmatian wines, and shop for traditional Croatian souvenirs.

B. Cultural Events:

Throughout the year, the palace hosts numerous cultural events, including music festivals, art exhibitions, and theatrical performances. These events add an extra layer of charm to an already captivating destination.

C. Riva Promenade:
Just outside the palace walls lies the Riva Promenade, a bustling waterfront area where visitors can take leisurely strolls, enjoy picturesque sunsets, and savor the laid-back Mediterranean atmosphere.

D. Marjan Hill:
For nature lovers and adventure seekers, a short hike up Marjan Hill rewards visitors with stunning panoramic views of Split and its surrounding landscapes.

4. Practical Information for Travelers:

A. Accommodation:
Split offers a wide range of accommodation options to suit all budgets. From luxurious hotels with sea views to cozy guesthouses tucked away in quiet alleys, travelers can find the perfect place to rest and recharge after a day of exploration.

B. Getting Around:
Diocletian's Palace is located in the heart of Split, and many attractions are within walking distance. For more distant places, the city has an efficient

public transportation system, including buses and ferries.

C. Best Time to Visit:
The best time to visit Diocletian's Palace is during the shoulder seasons of spring (April to June) and autumn (September to October). The weather is pleasant, and tourist crowds are smaller compared to the peak summer months.

D. Guided Tours:
To fully appreciate the historical significance and architectural beauty of the palace, consider taking a guided tour. Knowledgeable guides can provide valuable insights and ensure that you don't miss any hidden gems.

Diocletian's Palace in Split, Croatia, is an exquisite blend of history, culture, and modern-day vibrancy. From its awe-inspiring architectural marvels to the bustling streets filled with cafes and shops, the palace offers a truly immersive experience for travelers. As one of Croatia's must-visit destinations, a journey to Diocletian's Palace is sure to leave an indelible mark on any traveler's heart, leaving them with memories to cherish for a lifetime.

Nearby Islands and Beaches

Nestled along the stunning Dalmatian Coast, Split is a gem of a city in Croatia that boasts a rich history, charming architecture, and a vibrant cultural scene. However, one of the main attractions of this picturesque destination lies just off its shores - the nearby islands and beaches that offer a paradise for travelers seeking sun, sea, and serenity. In this comprehensive Croatia travel guide, we will take you on a journey to discover the enchanting islands and pristine beaches surrounding Split. From lively and bustling hotspots to hidden oases of tranquility, these nearby islands and beaches provide an unforgettable experience for every type of traveler.

1. *Getting to Split, Croatia:*

Before we delve into the beautiful islands and beaches, let's start with the basics of reaching Split. Split is conveniently connected to various major cities and countries by air, train, and ferry services. The Split Airport welcomes international flights from major European cities, making it easy for travelers from around the world to access this coastal paradise.

2. *Exploring the Islands:*

2.1 Hvar Island:

Hvar, often referred to as the "Queen of the Dalmatian Islands," is a must-visit destination for anyone exploring the Split region. This island is renowned for its vibrant nightlife, exquisite lavender fields, and charming medieval architecture. Enjoy strolling through the narrow streets of Hvar Town, take in the panoramic views from the fortress above, and relax on the idyllic sandy beaches such as Dubovica and Zlatni Rat.

2.2 Brač Island:

Brač Island, the third-largest island in the Adriatic Sea, is famous for its radiant white limestone, which was used to construct notable structures like the White House in Washington, D.C. The Zlatni Rat beach, with its distinctive horn shape, is a symbol of Croatia's natural beauty. Explore the quaint fishing village of Bol and indulge in local delicacies like olive oil and lamb dishes.

2.3 Vis Island:

Vis is an island that stands out for its untouched beauty and laid-back ambiance. Formerly a military zone, it was closed to tourists until the late 1980s, preserving its pristine nature and authentic charm. Visit the enchanting Stiniva Cove, which can only be reached by sea, and marvel at the crystal-clear waters of the Blue Cave. Don't miss the opportunity to savor the island's delicious seafood and local wines.

2.4 Šolta Island:

Šolta is a small and peaceful island that offers a serene escape from the bustling mainland. Known for its olive oil production, the island invites visitors to explore its picturesque villages, such as Grohote and Stomorska. Take leisurely walks along the coast, discover secluded coves, and immerse yourself in the simple pleasures of island life.

3. Discovering Pristine Beaches:

3.1 Bačvice Beach:

Located just a short walk from Split's city center, Bačvice Beach is the most popular and easily accessible beach in the area. Its fine sand and shallow waters make it ideal for families with children. Additionally, the beach is famous for the traditional Croatian game of picigin, a unique form of water sports played in shallow waters.

3.2 Kašjuni Beach:

For a more tranquil beach experience, head to Kašjuni Beach, located in the Marjan Forest Park. Surrounded by lush Mediterranean vegetation, this pebble beach offers a peaceful retreat from the city buzz. It's a great spot for swimming and snorkeling, and you can find some hidden rocky spots to enjoy a moment of solitude.

3.3 Strožanac Beach:

If you're seeking a beach that combines natural beauty with modern amenities, Strožanac Beach in Podstrana is an excellent choice. The long sandy coastline is perfect for leisurely walks, and the beach is equipped with facilities like cafes, bars, and water sports rentals.

Split, Croatia, is more than just a city with historical sites and cultural treasures. Its proximity to a myriad of beautiful islands and beaches makes it an ideal destination for travelers seeking both urban exploration and natural wonders. From the lively nightlife of Hvar to the unspoiled beauty of Vis, the nearby islands offer a diverse range of experiences. The pristine beaches along the coast of Split provide endless opportunities for relaxation and fun in the sun. So, whether you're a history enthusiast, a nature lover, or a sun-seeker, Split and its neighboring islands have something to offer every traveler, making it a truly enchanting destination in Croatia.

•*Plitvice Lakes National Park*

Nestled in the heart of Croatia lies a natural wonder that captivates the imagination of every traveler who sets foot within its boundaries. Plitvice Lakes National Park, a UNESCO World Heritage site since 1979, is a breathtaking marvel of cascading waterfalls, crystal-clear lakes, lush greenery, and diverse wildlife. Located in the central part of the country, near the border with Bosnia and Herzegovina, this national park attracts visitors from all corners of the globe. With its unmatched beauty and unique features, Plitvice Lakes promises an unforgettable experience for nature enthusiasts, hikers, photographers, and anyone seeking a retreat from the hustle and bustle of modern life.

1. *The Natural Beauty of Plitvice Lakes National Park:*

Spanning over 73,000 acres, Plitvice Lakes National Park boasts 16 interconnected terraced lakes, each flowing into the other through a series of captivating waterfalls and cascades. The lakes are renowned for their striking colors, ranging from emerald green to azure blue, created by the interplay of sunlight and minerals present in the water. The lush surrounding forests, predominantly composed of beech, fir, and spruce trees, add to the park's ethereal charm, especially during the vibrant autumn foliage.

2. *The Lakes and Waterfalls:*

Plitvice Lakes is often divided into two sections: the Upper Lakes (Gornja Jezera) and the Lower Lakes (Donja Jezera). The Upper Lakes, located in the higher elevation, are characterized by smaller cascades and serene, mirrored pools that reflect the surrounding vegetation. As visitors descend through wooden pathways and boardwalks, they will encounter the Lower Lakes, with their larger and more powerful waterfalls, such as Veliki Slap (Great Waterfall) and Milanovacki Slap.

3. Exploring the Park:

To preserve the park's fragile ecosystem, visitors are required to follow designated walking paths and boardwalks. The well-maintained trails offer an intimate encounter with the natural beauty of the park while safeguarding its delicate flora and fauna. There are various routes to choose from, catering to different fitness levels and time constraints, ranging from leisurely strolls to more challenging hikes that cover the entire park.

4. Boat Rides and Electric Trains:

Complementing the walking trails, boat rides are available on Lake Kozjak, the largest and deepest lake in the park. The boat ride provides an opportunity to admire the lakes and waterfalls from a different perspective and enjoy the tranquility of the surrounding landscape. Additionally, electric trains are available for visitors who wish to cover larger distances without walking extensively.

5. Flora and Fauna:

Plitvice Lakes National Park is home to a diverse array of flora and fauna, making it a haven for nature lovers and wildlife enthusiasts. The forests harbor an abundance of plant species, including some rare and endemic ones. The park is also inhabited by various animal species, such as brown bears, wolves, lynxes, deer, boars, and numerous bird species. Although elusive, lucky visitors may catch a glimpse of these magnificent creatures in their natural habitat.

6. The Importance of Conservation:

As a designated national park, Plitvice Lakes holds significant ecological and cultural value. The conservation efforts in the park are aimed at preserving its pristine condition, protecting endangered species, and maintaining the delicate balance of its ecosystem. Visitors are urged to adhere to the park's guidelines, such as not littering, staying on marked paths, and respecting the wildlife.

7. Best Time to Visit:

Plitvice Lakes National Park offers unique experiences throughout the year. Each season presents its own charm, but the peak tourist season typically falls between May and September when the weather is mild and the landscapes are at their greenest. Spring brings blooming flowers and lush vegetation, while autumn dazzles visitors with its golden hues. Winter, although less crowded, transforms the park into a winter wonderland, with frozen waterfalls and snow-covered landscapes, offering a serene and magical ambiance.

8. Practical Tips for Visitors:

- Accommodation:There are several hotels and guesthouses near the park, as well as campsites for nature enthusiasts who prefer to be closer to the outdoors.

- Entrance Fees:Plitvice Lakes National Park charges an entrance fee, with different prices for adults, children, and students. The revenue generated from these fees goes towards the conservation and maintenance of the park.

- Weather and Clothing:Weather in the park can be unpredictable, so it's advisable to dress in layers and wear comfortable walking shoes. Be prepared for rain, especially during the wetter months.

- Picnic Areas: There are designated picnic areas within the park where visitors can enjoy a meal amidst the serene surroundings. However, it's essential to dispose of waste responsibly.

- Photography: Plitvice Lakes is a paradise for photographers. Don't forget to bring your camera to capture the stunning landscapes and wildlife.

9. Local Cuisine and Culture:

Exploring Croatia is incomplete without savoring its traditional cuisine and immersing yourself in the local culture. Nearby villages offer authentic Croatian dishes, such as cevapi (grilled minced meat), burek (savory pastry), and various seafood delicacies. You can also indulge in regional wines and liqueurs, further enriching your experience of the country's culinary heritage.

A visit to Plitvice Lakes National Park is nothing short of a transformative journey through nature's unparalleled beauty. As you wander through the lush greenery, stand in awe of the cascading waterfalls, and witness the vivid colors of the lakes, you'll feel a profound connection to the natural world. Plitvice Lakes is a testament to the significance of conservation efforts, and its preservation is a collective responsibility for the generations to come. Embrace the splendor of this Croatian gem, and it will undoubtedly leave an indelible mark on your soul, making your travel to Croatia an unforgettable experience.

Natural Wonders of Plitvice

Croatia, a mesmerizing country nestled on the Adriatic coast of Europe, is a land of diverse landscapes, rich history, and vibrant culture. Among its many treasures, one destination stands out as a true marvel of nature - the Plitvice Lakes National Park. Located in the heart of Croatia, this enchanting wonderland of cascading waterfalls, crystal-clear lakes, lush forests, and diverse wildlife is a must-visit for any nature enthusiast or traveler seeking an unforgettable experience. In this Croatia travel guide, we delve into the splendor of Plitvice Lakes, exploring its natural wonders, history, activities, and practical tips to make the most of your journey.

1. The Beauty of Plitvice Lakes

Plitvice Lakes National Park, established in 1949, is the oldest and largest national park in Croatia, covering an area of nearly 300 square kilometers. It is a UNESCO World Heritage site, recognized for its outstanding natural value and unique karst landscape. The park's centerpiece and primary attraction is its chain of 16 terraced lakes, interconnected by a series of captivating waterfalls that weave through dense forests and limestone cliffs.

2. A Symphony of Waterfalls

The breathtaking series of waterfalls are the soul of Plitvice Lakes National Park. Veliki Slap, the tallest waterfall in Croatia, is a commanding presence, plunging down an impressive 78 meters. The harmony of gushing waters, the symphony of sounds, and the mesmerizing play of light and shadow create an unforgettable experience for every visitor. The waterfalls' appearance changes with the seasons, each season adding its unique touch to this natural masterpiece.

3. Crystal-Clear Lakes

The lakes of Plitvice are renowned for their striking turquoise and emerald hues. The mineral-rich waters, a result of the park's unique geological features, create an ever-changing palette of colors, ranging from azure blue to vibrant green. Visitors have the opportunity to explore the lakes via wooden walkways and hiking trails, immersing themselves in this paradise of serenity.

4. The Karst Landscape

The park's karst landscape is a geological wonder, formed over thousands of years through the dissolution of limestone. The action of water on the limestone creates sinkholes, caves, and underground rivers, making Plitvice an exceptional showcase of karst topography. The natural processes that shaped the area have created a harmonious balance between the water, land, and flora, making it an ecosystem of immense ecological significance.

5. Flora and Fauna

Plitvice Lakes National Park is a sanctuary for a wide variety of flora and fauna. The pristine forests surrounding the lakes are home to beech, fir, and spruce trees, as well as rare plant species. Wildlife enthusiasts will be delighted by the opportunity to spot brown bears, wolves, lynxes, deer, and an array of bird species, including eagles and owls. It's essential to respect the park's wildlife and maintain a safe distance from any animals encountered during your visit.

6. Activities in Plitvice Lakes

Beyond simply admiring the natural wonders, Plitvice offers an array of activities that allow visitors to immerse themselves fully in the park's beauty.

Hiking and Walking Trails:The park boasts a network of well-maintained hiking trails and wooden boardwalks, providing visitors with a range of options for exploring the lakes and waterfalls. Whether you're a leisurely walker or an avid hiker, there are routes to suit all levels of fitness and time constraints.

Boat Tours:Boat excursions operate on some of the lakes, offering a unique perspective from the water's surface. These tours provide a different viewpoint of the waterfalls and allow visitors to enjoy the tranquil beauty of the lakes from a different perspective.

Cycling:For those who prefer cycling, there are designated cycling trails in the park and the surrounding area. Biking allows you to explore more extensive parts of the park and its surroundings while enjoying the fresh air and natural surroundings.

Photography:Plitvice Lakes is a photographer's paradise. The natural beauty and ever-changing landscapes make it an ideal location for capturing stunning images. Remember to bring your camera and take advantage of the numerous photo opportunities throughout the park.

Winter Activities: In the winter months, when the park transforms into a snowy wonderland, activities like cross-country skiing and snowshoeing become popular among visitors. The serene beauty of the snow-covered landscape adds a magical touch to the park's already breathtaking scenery.

7. Practical Tips for Visiting

To ensure you have a memorable and enjoyable visit to Plitvice Lakes National Park, consider these practical tips:

a) Timing and Seasons: The park can get crowded during peak tourist seasons. To avoid the crowds and fully appreciate the tranquility, consider visiting during the shoulder seasons of spring or autumn. Each season offers a unique experience, from the blooming flowers and lush greenery of spring to the vibrant colors of autumn foliage.

b) Comfortable Footwear:Wear comfortable and sturdy footwear suitable for walking on uneven terrain. The park's wooden walkways can be slippery, particularly during or after rainfall.

c) Bring Water and Snacks:Exploring the park can be a day-long adventure, so it's essential to carry enough water and snacks to keep yourself hydrated and energized.

d) Follow Park Rules: Respect the park's rules and regulations, including staying on designated paths, not feeding wildlife, and disposing of trash responsibly.

e) Accommodation:There are various accommodation options in the surrounding areas, ranging from hotels to private lodgings and campsites. Be sure to book in advance, especially during the high season.

f) Guided Tours:Consider joining a guided tour to learn more about the park's history, geology, and wildlife from knowledgeable guides.

Plitvice Lakes National Park in Croatia is a natural wonderland that captivates all who venture into its lush embrace. Its stunning waterfalls, crystal-clear lakes, and diverse flora and fauna make it a place of unparalleled beauty and ecological significance. Whether you're a nature lover, an adventure seeker, or a photography enthusiast, Plitvice Lakes offers an experience that will remain etched in your memory forever. Embrace the opportunity to connect with nature and witness the raw beauty of one of Croatia's most extraordinary treasures.

Hiking and Wildlife Viewing

Nestled in the heart of Croatia, Plitvice Lakes National Park is a true natural wonder. Encompassing a vast expanse of lush forests, cascading waterfalls, and sixteen interconnected lakes, it is a haven for outdoor enthusiasts and wildlife enthusiasts alike. With its breathtaking scenery and rich biodiversity, the park offers an unparalleled opportunity for hiking and wildlife viewing. This Croatia travel guide will take you on a journey through the beauty and splendor of Plitvice Lakes National Park, highlighting the best hiking trails and the diverse wildlife that calls this protected area home.

Overview of Plitvice Lakes National Park

Plitvice Lakes National Park, established in 1949, is Croatia's oldest and largest national park, covering an area of over 295 square kilometers. It lies in the central part of the country, between the Mala Kapela mountain range to the northwest and the Lička Plješivica plateau to the southeast. The park's centerpiece is its sixteen turquoise lakes, arranged in cascading tiers, connected by a series of waterfalls and rivulets, creating a stunning landscape that has earned it the nickname "Land of Falling Lakes."

The unique geology of the area, characterized by the deposition of travertine, a form of limestone, has given rise to the ever-evolving formations of the lakes and waterfalls. Over millennia, water from the Bijela and Crna rivers has carved its path through the porous rock, resulting in the captivating sights that visitors can witness today.

Hiking in Plitvice Lakes National Park

1. Lower Lakes Trail: This trail takes visitors on a mesmerizing journey around the lower lakes, providing up-close views of some of the most iconic waterfalls in the park, such as Veliki Slap, the tallest waterfall in Croatia. The trail is relatively easy, making it accessible to hikers of all levels. The wooden footbridges and well-maintained paths ensure a comfortable hike amid the enchanting surroundings of crystal-clear lakes and lush vegetation.

2. Upper Lakes Trail: For those seeking a more challenging hike, the Upper Lakes Trail offers a rewarding adventure. This trail meanders through dense forests and leads to the upper lakes, where visitors can witness the unique sight of water pouring from one lake into another. The vistas from the higher elevations are awe-inspiring, and the tranquility of the upper lakes adds to the allure of this trail.

3. Plitvica River Canyon Trail: This trail diverges from the main circuit and allows hikers to explore the less-frequented regions of the park. It follows the course of the Plitvica River, providing picturesque views of the canyon and its cascading waterfalls. This trail is an excellent option for those looking to escape the crowds and immerse themselves in the serene wilderness.

4. Kozjak Lake Trail: Kozjak is the largest and deepest lake in Plitvice Lakes National Park. The trail around Kozjak Lake is relatively easy and offers glimpses of the lake's vibrant colors, reflections of the surrounding cliffs, and opportunities to spot various bird species that inhabit the area.

5. Great Waterfall Trail: As the name suggests, this trail leads visitors to the Great Waterfall, another magnificent cascade in the park. The trail encompasses diverse terrain, and while not the

easiest, the reward of witnessing the impressive waterfall up close makes it a popular choice for many hikers.

Wildlife Viewing in Plitvice Lakes National Park

Plitvice Lakes National Park is not only renowned for its stunning landscapes but also for its diverse wildlife. The park's protected status has allowed numerous species to thrive in their natural habitats, making it a haven for wildlife enthusiasts. Some of the wildlife you might encounter during your visit include:

1. Brown Bears: Plitvice is home to a population of brown bears, though spotting them can be challenging due to their elusive nature. Visitors are more likely to see signs of their presence, such as footprints and claw marks on trees.

2. European Lynx: The park is also home to the elusive and solitary European lynx. These magnificent felines are rarely seen, as they are skilled at avoiding human contact.

3. Red Deer: The largest land mammal in Croatia, the red deer, can be found roaming the park's forests. They are most active during dusk and dawn, so early morning or late evening hikes increase the chances of spotting them.

4. Wild Boars: Wild boars are relatively common in the park, and they are more active during the night. Keep an eye out for their distinctive tracks and wallows in the mud.

5. Wolves: Though rarely seen, wolves also inhabit the park's remote areas. They play a crucial role in the park's ecosystem, contributing to a healthy balance among species.

6. Birds: Plitvice Lakes National Park is a birdwatcher's paradise, with over 120 bird species recorded in the area. Some of the notable species include golden eagles, peregrine falcons, white-throated dippers, and various waterfowl.

Tips for Wildlife Viewing

1. Be Patient and Quiet: Wildlife spotting requires patience and silence. Move slowly and avoid making loud noises that may scare away the animals.

2. Use Binoculars and Telephoto Lenses: To observe wildlife from a distance without disturbing them, bring binoculars or telephoto camera lenses.

3. Respect Wildlife and Their Habitat: Keep a safe distance from the animals and refrain from feeding them. Respect their natural behaviors and habitats to ensure their well-being.

4. Follow Park Guidelines: Plitvice Lakes National Park has specific rules and guidelines to protect the wildlife and environment. Adhere to these regulations for a responsible and sustainable visit.

Plitvice Lakes National Park is a true gem of Croatia, offering a captivating blend of hiking adventures and wildlife encounters. The park's network of trails allows visitors to explore its enchanting lakes, waterfalls, and diverse landscapes, while the protected status ensures the preservation of its remarkable wildlife. Whether you're an avid hiker, a wildlife enthusiast, or simply a lover of natural beauty, Plitvice Lakes National Park is a must-visit destination that will leave you with memories to cherish for a lifetime. As you venture into this pristine wilderness, remember to tread lightly, respect the flora and fauna, and savor every moment of this extraordinary Croatian experience.

CHAPTER FOUR

Hidden Gems and Off-the-Beaten-Path

Istrian Peninsula

Nestled along the Adriatic Sea in Croatia, the Istrian Peninsula is a captivating region renowned for its stunning landscapes, rich history, mouthwatering cuisine, and warm hospitality. This guide aims to provide a comprehensive overview of the Istrian Peninsula as a must-visit destination for travelers in search of a unique and unforgettable experience. From historical sites to pristine beaches, from vibrant cities to charming villages, Istria offers a diverse range of attractions that will leave every visitor enchanted.

1. Geography and Location:
The Istrian Peninsula is located in the northwestern part of Croatia, jutting out into the Adriatic Sea. It is bordered by Slovenia to the northwest, the Kvarner Gulf to the east, and the Gulf of Trieste to the west. The region covers an area of approximately 3,476 square miles (9,000 square kilometers) and is characterized by its hilly terrain, lush green landscapes, and a coastline that stretches for over 350 miles (560 kilometers).

2. Historical Significance:

Istria boasts a fascinating history that dates back to prehistoric times. The region has been influenced and ruled by various civilizations, including the Illyrians, Romans, Venetians, and Austro-Hungarians, each leaving their mark on the local culture and architecture. Traces of the past can be found in the numerous Roman ruins, medieval hilltop towns, and Venetian-influenced coastal cities.

3. Top Destinations in Istria:

a. Pula:Pula is the largest city in Istria and is renowned for its well-preserved Roman amphitheater, known as the Pula Arena. This ancient amphitheater is one of the best-preserved in the world and serves as a testament to the Roman influence in the region. Visitors can also explore the Temple of Augustus, the Arch of Sergii, and the charming old town with its narrow streets and vibrant atmosphere.

b. Rovinj:Often described as one of the most picturesque towns in the Mediterranean, Rovinj captivates visitors with its colorful houses, cobblestone streets, and charming fishing harbor. The St. Euphemia Church, located on a hill overlooking the town, offers panoramic views of the surrounding area.

c. Motovun: This medieval hilltop town is perched on a hill overlooking the Mirna River valley. Motovun is famous for its truffles, and visitors can enjoy truffle-hunting excursions and indulge in truffle-infused dishes at local restaurants. The annual Motovun Film Festival also attracts cinephiles from around the world.

d. Poreč:Poreč is a coastal town known for its Euphrasian Basilica, a UNESCO World Heritage Site. The basilica features stunning Byzantine mosaics and is a remarkable example of early Christian art and architecture.

4. Cultural Attractions:
Istria's cultural heritage is showcased through numerous events, festivals, and traditions that take place throughout the year. The region's rich folklore, music, dance, and culinary traditions are celebrated during various festivals and cultural gatherings, providing visitors with an authentic insight into Istria's vibrant cultural identity.

a. Istrian Wine and Gastronomy:Istria is a gastronomic paradise, and its cuisine is heavily influenced by Italian, Austrian, and Croatian traditions. Olive oil, truffles, seafood, and Istrian wines are some of the region's culinary highlights. Travelers can visit local wineries to taste Malvasia, Teran, and other indigenous wines while savoring traditional dishes at local konobas (taverns).

b. Istrian Festivals: Istria hosts numerous festivals, celebrating everything from wine and truffles to music and film. The Pula Film Festival, the Truffle Days in Buzet, and the International Festival of Dance and Non-Verbal Theater in Svetvinčenat are just a few examples of the diverse events that showcase the region's cultural richness.

5. Natural Wonders:
Istria's natural beauty is as diverse as its history and culture. From crystal-clear waters to lush green landscapes, the region offers an abundance of outdoor activities for nature enthusiasts.

a. Brijuni National Park: Situated off the southwestern coast of Istria, the Brijuni Islands are a stunning archipelago known for their diverse flora and fauna. The national park offers guided tours that include visits to ancient Roman ruins and the former residence of Yugoslavia's President Tito.

b. Cape Kamenjak: Located at the southernmost tip of Istria, Cape Kamenjak is a protected nature reserve featuring rugged cliffs, hidden coves, and pristine beaches. It is an ideal spot for hiking, cycling, and swimming.

6. Outdoor Activities:
The varied landscape of Istria provides ample opportunities for outdoor enthusiasts to engage in various activities.

a. Water Sports: The clear waters of the Adriatic Sea make Istria a perfect destination for water sports such as sailing, diving, and windsurfing.

b. Cycling: Istria offers a well-developed network of cycling routes that lead through picturesque countryside, vineyards, and coastal areas, catering to cyclists of all levels.

c. Hiking and Trekking: Numerous hiking trails crisscross Istria, taking travelers through lush forests, scenic viewpoints, and historic sites.

7. *Accommodation and Transportation:*
Istria offers a wide range of accommodation options, from luxury hotels to budget-friendly guesthouses and cozy agritourism farms. Coastal cities like Pula and Rovinj have excellent hotel infrastructure, while smaller towns and villages offer a more authentic and intimate experience.

Transportation within Istria is convenient, with an extensive network of buses connecting major towns and cities. Renting a car is recommended for those who wish to explore the region's more remote areas and countryside at their own pace.

The Istrian Peninsula in Croatia is a treasure trove of history, culture, natural beauty, and culinary delights. Whether you are interested in ancient Roman ruins, charming coastal towns, lush landscapes, or delicious local cuisine, Istria has something to offer every traveler. This comprehensive travel guide should provide you with the essential information to plan an unforgettable journey to this enchanting region and create memories that will last a lifetime. So pack your bags, immerse yourself in Istria's unique charm, and let the magic of this Croatian gem unfold before your eyes.

Pula - Roman Amphitheater

Nestled on the Istrian Peninsula in Croatia lies the ancient city of Pula, boasting a rich historical legacy dating back to the Roman era. One of its most remarkable and iconic landmarks is the Pula Roman Amphitheater, also known as the Pula Arena. This well-preserved ancient amphitheater stands as a testament to the region's illustrious past and serves as a major draw for tourists and history enthusiasts from all over the world. In this Croatia travel guide, we embark on an adventure to uncover the grandeur of Pula's Roman Amphitheater, delving into its history, architecture, cultural significance, and the experience of visiting this awe-inspiring monument.

A Glimpse into Pula's History and Location

Pula, situated in the southwestern part of the Istrian Peninsula, boasts a strategic coastal position along the Adriatic Sea. Its history can be traced back to ancient times when it was inhabited by the Illyrians. However, it was under Roman rule that the city truly flourished, earning its place as an essential maritime and administrative center. The amphitheater, constructed during the 1st century AD, served as a hub for entertainment, hosting gladiator battles, public spectacles, and various cultural events. Today, Pula proudly stands as one of the most culturally and historically significant cities in Croatia.

The Pula Roman Amphitheater - A Marvel of Roman Architecture

1. Architecture and Design: The Pula Roman Amphitheater showcases an exemplary display of Roman architecture. Built during the reign of Emperor Vespasian, it is one of the best-preserved amphitheaters in the world. The structure was constructed using local limestone, boasting an elliptical shape with dimensions of approximately 132 meters in length and 105 meters in width. Its outer walls reach heights of up to 32 meters, accentuated by three rows of arches, Doric, Ionic, and Corinthian in style, providing insight into the Roman influence on architecture.

2. Capacity and Spectacles: The amphitheater could accommodate around 23,000 spectators during its heyday. These spectators gathered to witness a variety of events, including gladiator battles, animal hunts, reenactments of famous battles, and

theatrical performances. The atmosphere would have been electrifying, as the Roman citizens reveled in the grandeur of the spectacles unfolding before them.

Cultural Significance and Preservation

1. A Window to the Past: The Pula Roman Amphitheater serves as a living museum, offering visitors a unique opportunity to step back in time and experience the glory of ancient Roman civilization. Its well-preserved state and continued use for modern events, such as concerts and festivals, showcase its cultural significance and relevance through the ages.

2. Preservation Efforts: Over the centuries, the amphitheater has undergone various alterations and adaptations. During the medieval period, it was repurposed for housing, workshops, and even a fortress. However, in the 19th century, efforts to restore and preserve the amphitheater began, recognizing its historical importance. Today, it is managed by the Pula Film Festival, which showcases films under the starlit skies of this ancient marvel.

The Pula Roman Amphitheater Experience

1. Visiting the Amphitheater: When visiting Pula, the Roman Amphitheater is an absolute must-see. As you approach the colossal structure, a sense of

awe and wonder is inevitable. The magnitude of the amphitheater becomes apparent, and its impressive façade leaves visitors astounded.

2. Guided Tours: To truly appreciate the historical and architectural significance of the amphitheater, guided tours are available. Knowledgeable guides take visitors on a journey through time, recounting tales of gladiators, emperors, and the enthralling events that once unfolded within the arena's walls.

3. Spectacular Views: Climbing to the top tiers of the amphitheater rewards visitors with breathtaking panoramic views of Pula and the surrounding landscape. The sweeping vistas over the Adriatic Sea add to the magic of the experience.

4. Events and Festivals: Depending on the time of your visit, you might have the chance to witness various events and festivals hosted within the amphitheater. From cultural performances to music concerts, these events add a contemporary touch to the ancient venue.

Exploring Pula - Beyond the Amphitheater

1. Historic Sites: Pula is replete with historical sites that warrant exploration. The Arch of Sergii, Temple of Augustus, and the Pula Forum are just a few of the other Roman remnants that await your discovery.

2. Cuisine and Gastronomy: No visit to Croatia is complete without savoring its delectable cuisine. Pula offers an array of restaurants and eateries where you can indulge in local delicacies, including seafood specialties, truffles, and Istrian wine.

3. Nature and Beaches: The Istrian Peninsula is blessed with stunning natural landscapes and pristine beaches. Take a break from history to enjoy the beauty of places like Kamenjak Nature Reserve and Verudela Beach.

A trip to Pula, Croatia, is a journey through time, and the Pula Roman Amphitheater stands as its most awe-inspiring relic. Its grandeur and historical significance make it a must-visit destination for anyone traveling to Croatia, especially for those with an interest in ancient Roman civilization. Beyond the amphitheater, Pula offers a delightful blend of history, culture, and natural beauty, providing a truly enriching experience for every traveler. So, pack your bags and embark on an adventure to Pula to witness the splendor of this remarkable Roman Amphitheater and explore the treasures of the Istrian Peninsula.

Rovinj - Charming Coastal Town

Welcome to Rovinj, a picturesque coastal town located on the Istrian Peninsula in Croatia. Known for its stunning natural beauty, rich history, and vibrant cultural heritage, Rovinj has become a favorite destination for travelers seeking an authentic Mediterranean experience. This comprehensive travel guide will take you on a journey through Rovinj's past and present, uncovering its top attractions, activities, cuisine, and accommodation options, ensuring that your visit to this charming town will be nothing short of extraordinary.

1. A Brief History of Rovinj

Rovinj's history dates back to prehistoric times when it was inhabited by the Illyrians, an ancient civilization. Over the centuries, it experienced the influence of various civilizations, including the Romans, Byzantines, Venetians, and Austro-Hungarians. These cultural influences are evident in the town's architecture, art, and traditions.

During the Venetian rule, Rovinj flourished as an important maritime and fishing center, evident in its picturesque harbor and narrow cobbled streets. In 1797, the town fell under the rule of the Austro-Hungarian Empire until 1918 when it became part of Italy. After World War II, Rovinj was annexed to Yugoslavia, and eventually, it became a part of the independent Republic of Croatia in the early 1990s.

2. *Exploring Rovinj's Old Town*

The heart of Rovinj lies in its charming old town, a maze of narrow streets lined with colorful Venetian-style buildings. Begin your exploration at the main square, Trg Maršala Tita, where you'll find the impressive Baroque Church of St. Euphemia. Climb the bell tower for panoramic views of the town and the sparkling Adriatic Sea.

Stroll along Grisia Street, famous for its vibrant art scene and numerous galleries showcasing the works of local artists. The Balbi Arch, a well-preserved Roman arch dating back to the 17th century, marks the entrance to the old town and is a must-see historical landmark.

3. *Rovinj's Natural Beauty*

Rovinj boasts some of the most stunning natural landscapes on the Istrian Peninsula. The town is nestled on a small peninsula, and wherever you go, you'll be treated to breathtaking views of the crystal-clear waters of the Adriatic Sea. Explore the rocky coastline, discover hidden coves, and relax on pebble beaches surrounded by lush Mediterranean vegetation.

A must-visit spot is the Golden Cape Forest Park, known locally as "Zlatni Rt." This lush green oasis offers numerous walking and cycling trails, perfect for nature enthusiasts. The Punta Corrente Park is also a popular spot for picnics and leisurely walks, with its rich biodiversity and fragrant pine forests.

4. Rovinj's Top Attractions

Aside from the old town and natural beauty, Rovinj offers a range of attractions for every interest. The Rovinj Heritage Museum provides insight into the town's history and showcases a diverse collection of artifacts. For art lovers, the Batana Eco-Museum offers a unique glimpse into the traditional way of life of Rovinj's fishermen.

For a taste of local life, visit the daily fish market on the waterfront, where you can buy freshly caught seafood and experience the vibrant atmosphere of the local community. The nearby Monkodonja archaeological site is a fascinating prehistoric hillfort that sheds light on Rovinj's ancient past.

5. Outdoor Activities and Adventures

Rovinj is an outdoor enthusiast's paradise, offering a plethora of activities and adventures. Explore the underwater world of the Adriatic Sea through snorkeling or scuba diving excursions, revealing an array of marine life and underwater caves.

Adventurous souls can indulge in various water sports such as kayaking, windsurfing, and paddleboarding. Additionally, sailing tours are available, providing an opportunity to explore the nearby islands and secluded bays.

Cycling is a popular activity in Rovinj, with well-marked bike paths leading through picturesque landscapes and charming villages. For hikers, the nearby Učka Nature Park offers various trails with stunning vistas over the Adriatic coastline.

6. Gastronomy in Rovinj

No travel guide to Rovinj would be complete without mentioning its delectable cuisine. With its coastal location, Rovinj is renowned for its fresh seafood, particularly shellfish and fish dishes cooked with locally sourced olive oil and aromatic herbs. Try the Istrian pasta dishes such as "fuži" and "pljukanci," often served with truffles, another delicacy the region is famous for.

To complement your meal, indulge in local wines, particularly the Malvasia and Teran varieties, both deeply rooted in Istrian winemaking traditions. For a sweet finish, sample some traditional Istrian desserts like "fritule" or "kroštule," small fried pastries sprinkled with powdered sugar.

7. Accommodation Options in Rovinj

Rovinj offers a diverse range of accommodation options to suit every budget and preference. From luxurious hotels overlooking the sea to cozy guesthouses in the heart of the old town, you'll find something that fits your needs. Alternatively, immerse yourself in the local culture by staying at one of the family-run agritourism farms in the countryside, where you can savor homemade meals and experience Istrian hospitality.

Rovinj, a charming coastal town on the Istrian Peninsula in Croatia, captivates visitors with its unique blend of history, culture, and natural beauty. From its cobbled streets and colorful Venetian-style buildings to its breathtaking coastline and gastronomic delights, Rovinj promises an unforgettable travel experience.

As you explore this enchanting town, take the time to immerse yourself in its rich history, indulge in the local cuisine, and partake in the numerous outdoor activities on offer. Whether you seek relaxation, adventure, or cultural exploration, Rovinj is sure to leave a lasting impression and become a cherished memory of your journey through Croatia's captivating landscapes.

•Zadar

Welcome to Zadar, a hidden gem tucked away on Croatia's stunning Adriatic coast. With its rich history, picturesque landscapes, and vibrant culture, Zadar offers an enchanting experience for every traveler. In this Croatia travel guide, we will delve deep into the wonders of Zadar, providing you with an extensive overview of its history, attractions, cuisine, accommodations, and more. Whether you are an adventurer seeking natural beauty or a history enthusiast keen to unravel the city's past, Zadar promises to captivate your heart and soul.

1. History and Culture:

Zadar boasts a storied history that dates back thousands of years, with influences from Roman, Byzantine, Venetian, and Croatian cultures. Once a major Roman city, the remnants of its ancient past can still be witnessed in the Old Town. Among its most iconic historical sites is the Roman Forum, an impressive archaeological site where you can walk among the ruins of ancient temples and public buildings.

Zadar's rich cultural heritage is evident in its numerous churches, including the famous St. Donatus' Church, a symbol of the city and a prime example of Byzantine architecture. The Cathedral of St. Anastasia, with its intricate facade and ornate interior, is another must-visit religious site.

2. Landmarks and Attractions:

Zadar's unique blend of ancient history and contemporary innovation makes it an exciting destination for travelers. A remarkable modern attraction is the Sea Organ, an architectural marvel that uses the power of the sea to create soothing, harmonious sounds. Nearby, the Sun Salutation is a large, illuminated solar-powered installation that comes alive with colorful lights after dark.

Taking a stroll along Zadar's waterfront promenade, the Riva, allows visitors to enjoy breathtaking views of the Adriatic Sea while experiencing the city's lively atmosphere. The Land Gate, part of the city's medieval fortifications, offers a glimpse into Zadar's defensive past.

The Museum of Ancient Glass is a hidden gem that exhibits an extensive collection of ancient glass artifacts found in the area, giving visitors insight into the region's craftsmanship and trade during the Roman period.

3. Nature and Adventure:

Zadar's natural beauty is nothing short of awe-inspiring. The nearby Kornati National Park is a paradise for nature lovers, boasting an archipelago of 89 uninhabited islands and islets adorned with rugged cliffs and crystal-clear waters. Boat excursions to the Kornati Islands offer a chance to explore these unspoiled wonders and enjoy some of the best diving spots in Croatia.

For an unforgettable experience, visit the Plitvice Lakes National Park, a couple of hours' drive from Zadar. This UNESCO World Heritage site is a wonderland of cascading waterfalls, lush forests, and interconnected lakes of vibrant turquoise and emerald hues.

Adventure enthusiasts can indulge in activities such as hiking, cycling, and rock climbing in the nearby Velebit Mountains, which offer mesmerizing vistas of the Adriatic coastline.

4. *Culinary Delights:*

Croatian cuisine is a delightful fusion of Mediterranean and continental flavors, and Zadar is no exception. Fresh seafood, locally produced olive oil, and a variety of cheeses are prominent features of the region's gastronomic offerings. Head to the bustling Zadar Market to savor seasonal fruits, vegetables, and traditional delicacies.

Indulge in a plate of black cuttlefish risotto, a regional specialty that showcases the Adriatic's bounty. Paired with a glass of local wine or the renowned Maraschino liqueur made from the marasca cherry, this culinary experience will leave a lasting impression.

5. Festivals and Events:

Zadar comes alive with festivals and events throughout the year. The Zadar Summer Theater Festival (Zadarsko Ljeto) brings a vibrant array of open-air performances, including theater, concerts, and dance, against the stunning backdrop of historical landmarks.

The Kalelarga Street Festival celebrates the city's main thoroughfare with a mix of arts, crafts, and traditional music, providing a glimpse into Zadar's lively cultural scene.

6. Accommodations:

Zadar offers a wide range of accommodations to suit every budget and taste. From luxurious waterfront hotels with stunning views to cozy guesthouses nestled in the heart of the Old Town, you'll find the perfect place to call home during your stay.

As you immerse yourself in the wonders of Zadar, you'll discover a city that seamlessly blends its rich history with modern creativity. From ancient Roman ruins to contemporary architectural wonders, from pristine natural landscapes to culinary delights, Zadar is a destination that promises an unforgettable travel experience.

Embrace the warm hospitality of the locals, indulge in the vibrant culture, and let the beauty of Zadar cast its spell on you. As you bid farewell to this charming city, you'll carry with you cherished memories of a journey that has touched your heart in ways you never imagined.

Sea Organ and Sun Salutation

Nestled on the Dalmatian coast of Croatia, the city of Zadar is a hidden gem waiting to be explored by avid travelers. Rich in history, culture, and natural beauty, Zadar offers a plethora of attractions for visitors to immerse themselves in the unique Croatian charm. Two must-visit landmarks that stand out in this ancient city are the Sea Organ and Sun Salutation. These modern art installations showcase the harmonious blend of art, nature, and technology, leaving visitors in awe of the city's innovative spirit. This Croatia travel guide will take you on a journey to explore the fascinating Sea Organ and Sun Salutation in Zadar, providing you with everything you need to know for an unforgettable experience.

I. Zadar: A Historical and Cultural Hub

Before we delve into the enchanting attractions, let's familiarize ourselves with the allure of Zadar. With a history that spans thousands of years, Zadar boasts a rich tapestry of cultures, including Roman,

Byzantine, Venetian, and Ottoman influences. The city's historical center is a treasure trove of well-preserved Roman ruins, medieval churches, and charming cobblestone streets that invite visitors to wander and get lost in time. The unique blend of ancient and modern architecture offers a captivating visual contrast, and it is within this vibrant setting that the Sea Organ and Sun Salutation find their home.

II. The Sea Organ: A Symphony of Nature and Sound

The Sea Organ, known locally as "Morske Orgulje," is a marvel of contemporary art and engineering. Located along the Zadar waterfront, this extraordinary musical instrument interacts directly with the natural forces of the Adriatic Sea, producing an ethereal symphony of sounds.

Designed by Croatian architect Nikola Bašić, the Sea Organ is composed of a series of marble steps that descend into the sea. Beneath these steps, a network of narrow channels and resonating cavities has been ingeniously integrated. As the sea's waves lap against the steps, air is pushed into the cavities, causing musical notes to emanate from concealed openings.

The result is a mesmerizing soundscape that evolves with the tides and the intensity of the waves. Locals and visitors alike gather here at different times of the day to witness the enchanting performance. The Sea Organ not only invites reflection and relaxation but also fosters a profound connection with the natural world and its ever-changing rhythms.

III. Sun Salutation: A Dance of Light

Adjacent to the Sea Organ, another remarkable art installation awaits discovery. The Sun Salutation, or "Pozdrav Suncu," is an interactive lighting installation that celebrates the sun's beauty and energy. Designed by the same architect, Nikola Bašić, this circular installation consists of 300 multi-layered glass plates embedded into the pavement.

During the day, the glass plates absorb solar energy, and as the sun sets, the magic begins. The Sun Salutation transforms into a breathtaking display of colors and patterns, illuminating the waterfront promenade with a dance of light. The ever-changing light show mirrors the spectacle of a sunset, captivating spectators with its radiant beauty.

Travelers are encouraged to take a seat on the smooth glass surface and witness the spectacle unfold around them. The experience is awe-inspiring, as the setting sun and the play of light merge to create an unforgettable visual symphony.

IV. A Day in Zadar: Exploring the Sea Organ and Sun Salutation

To make the most of your visit to the Sea Organ and Sun Salutation, plan a day of exploration around these landmarks.

1. Morning: Exploring the Historical Center
Start your day by immersing yourself in Zadar's rich history. Wander through the ancient streets of the Old Town, marvel at the well-preserved Roman Forum, and visit the remarkable St. Donatus Church. As you stroll along the streets, you'll encounter charming cafes and shops, offering the perfect opportunity to indulge in some local delicacies and souvenirs.

2. Afternoon: Relaxing by the Sea Organ
Head to the waterfront and find a spot along the marble steps of the Sea Organ. Take in the soothing sounds of the sea and let yourself be carried away by the melodies produced by this unique instrument. The Sea Organ's music changes with the tides and wind, offering a distinct experience at each visit.

3. Sunset: Admiring the Sun Salutation
As the day draws to a close, position yourself at the center of the Sun Salutation to witness the sun's majestic descent into the horizon. The evolving light display around you will add a touch of magic to this picturesque moment. Capture the

captivating scenes on camera or simply immerse yourself in the ambiance of the setting sun.

4. Evening: Dining by the Waterfront
End your day in Zadar with a delightful dinner by the sea. Several restaurants along the waterfront offer a selection of fresh seafood and traditional Croatian dishes. Savor the local flavors as you bask in the memories of your day's adventures.

V. *Practical Information*

1. How to Get There
Zadar is well-connected by air, road, and sea. Zadar International Airport serves numerous destinations, making it easily accessible from various European cities. Additionally, trains and buses connect Zadar to other major Croatian cities, and there are regular ferry services to nearby islands and towns.

2. Best Time to Visit
Zadar experiences a Mediterranean climate, with warm summers and mild winters. The best time to visit is during the shoulder seasons of spring (April to June) and autumn (September to October) when the weather is pleasant, and the tourist crowds are thinner.

3. Accommodation Options
Zadar offers a wide range of accommodation options to suit different budgets and preferences.

The Old Town has charming boutique hotels and guesthouses, while modern hotels can be found along the waterfront and in surrounding areas.

4. Nearby Attractions

While in Zadar, consider exploring the nearby Plitvice Lakes National Park, a UNESCO World Heritage site renowned for its cascading waterfalls and crystal-clear lakes. Additionally, the Kornati Islands, a national park consisting of 89 stunning islands, are easily accessible from Zadar and are a paradise for nature lovers.

Zadar's Sea Organ and Sun Salutation are not only captivating works of art but also powerful symbols of the city's identity as a hub of culture, creativity, and innovation. A visit to these attractions is a unique opportunity to connect with nature, experience the power of art and technology, and immerse oneself in the poetic beauty of the Dalmatian coast. As you leave Zadar with unforgettable memories, you'll find that the harmonious blend of ancient history and modern ingenuity has left an indelible mark on your heart, drawing you back to this enchanting Croatian city time and again.

Historic Sites and Museums

Nestled along the stunning Adriatic coastline, Zadar is a gem among Croatia's historical and cultural destinations. This ancient city, with its rich history dating back to prehistoric times, offers visitors a remarkable blend of architectural wonders, well-preserved heritage sites, and world-class museums. In this travel guide, we'll take you on an exciting journey through Zadar's historic sites and museums, uncovering the stories and significance of each location.

1. Zadar's Historical Heritage:

1.1 The Roman Forum:
Our journey through time begins at the Roman Forum, located in the heart of the city. As the largest forum on the eastern Adriatic coast, it served as the central hub of public life in ancient Zadar. Today, visitors can marvel at well-preserved ruins, Corinthian columns, and remnants of temples, highlighting the city's Roman past.

1.2 St. Donatus Church:
This remarkable circular church, believed to have been built in the 9th century, is a masterpiece of Byzantine architecture. Its distinct shape and robust structure stand as a testament to the city's early Christian heritage.

1.3 St. Anastasia's Cathedral:
A short walk from the Roman Forum takes you to St. Anastasia's Cathedral, the largest cathedral in Dalmatia. Built in the 12th and 13th centuries, this impressive Romanesque cathedral boasts stunning

architecture, religious artifacts, and a captivating history.

1.4 Land Gate and City Walls:
Zadar's fortified walls and gates served as a formidable defense against various invaders throughout its history. The Land Gate, built in the 16th century, is a prominent entrance to the old town and a symbol of the city's resilience.

2. *Museums in Zadar:*

2.1 Archaeological Museum:
For history enthusiasts, the Archaeological Museum in Zadar is a treasure trove of artifacts that depict the city's past. From prehistoric remains to Roman antiquities, this museum offers a comprehensive insight into the region's archaeological significance.

2.2 Museum of Ancient Glass:
Zadar has a unique cultural attraction in the Museum of Ancient Glass. Showcasing an extensive collection of ancient glassware discovered in the region, visitors can witness the exquisite craftsmanship of glassblowers from centuries ago.

2.3 Zadar National Museum:
The Zadar National Museum, located in the 16th-century building of the Convent of St. Mary, houses an impressive collection of religious art, historical documents, and cultural artifacts,

providing a deeper understanding of Croatia's cultural and religious heritage.

2.4 Museum of Illusions:
For a fun and interactive experience, the Museum of Illusions in Zadar is a must-visit. This engaging museum offers mind-bending optical illusions, holograms, and puzzles, creating an entertaining experience for visitors of all ages.

3. Contemporary Attractions:

3.1 Sea Organ:
One of Zadar's most innovative modern attractions is the Sea Organ. Designed by architect Nikola Bašić, this unique installation transforms the natural waves of the Adriatic Sea into melodic sounds, creating a harmonious blend of nature and music.

3.2 Greeting to the Sun:
Adjacent to the Sea Organ is the Greeting to the Sun, an impressive light installation also designed by Nikola Bašić. As the sun sets, the circular solar-powered installation illuminates in various colors, providing a mesmerizing visual display.

4. Day Trips from Zadar:

4.1 Kornati National Park:
Embark on a boat trip to Kornati National Park, an archipelago of 89 stunning islands, islets, and reefs.

The park's diverse marine life, crystal-clear waters, and rugged landscapes make it a paradise for nature lovers and divers.

4.2 Plitvice Lakes National Park:
Venture further inland to the enchanting Plitvice Lakes National Park, a UNESCO World Heritage site renowned for its interconnected lakes, waterfalls, and lush greenery. It's a haven for hikers, photographers, and wildlife enthusiasts.

Zadar is an ideal destination for history aficionados and culture enthusiasts alike. Its historic sites and museums offer a glimpse into Croatia's captivating past, while its modern attractions showcase the city's progressive spirit. As you explore the rich heritage of Zadar, you'll be immersed in the tapestry of its history, leaving you with memories that will last a lifetime. So, plan your visit to Zadar, Croatia, and embark on a journey through time in this remarkable city of antiquity and charm.

•*Korcula Island*

Croatia, with its stunning coastline along the Adriatic Sea, is a land of diverse natural beauty, historical wonders, and picturesque islands. Among these idyllic islands, Korčula stands out as a gem awaiting discovery. Located in the southern part of Croatia, Korčula Island offers a perfect blend of rich history, captivating culture, and pristine landscapes that will leave any traveler in awe. This comprehensive travel guide will take you on a journey through the enchanting allure of Korčula Island, as you explore its historical sites, indulge in its delicious cuisine, bask in its breathtaking beaches, and immerse yourself in its unique local traditions.

I. Historical Overview:

Korčula Island boasts a rich and storied history that dates back to ancient times. The island's origins are intertwined with Greek settlers, followed by the Illyrians and Romans, who left their marks on its landscape and culture. However, it is the Venetian influence that remains most prominent, evident in the charming architecture and labyrinthine streets of its main town, also called Korčula.

A. Korčula Town:

The heart of the island, Korčula Town, is a walled medieval gem. Enclosed by impressive stone fortifications, the town is reminiscent of a mini-Dubrovnik, with its red-tiled roofs and narrow cobblestone streets. St. Mark's Cathedral, a stunning Gothic-Renaissance structure, stands proudly in the town center, displaying remarkable artworks and religious relics. The Marco Polo House is another highlight, believed to be the birthplace of the famed explorer.

B. The Legend of Marco Polo:

Korčula Island proudly claims Marco Polo as its native son, and a museum dedicated to the explorer showcases his adventurous life and journeys to the Far East. Whether or not Marco Polo was indeed born on the island remains a subject of debate, but the legend adds an extra layer of intrigue to Korčula's historical significance.

II. Culture and Traditions:

Korčula's cultural heritage is deeply rooted in its seafaring past and is celebrated through various traditions and events.

A. Moreska Sword Dance:

The Moreska Sword Dance is a captivating reenactment of a medieval battle between the Red King and the Black King over a kidnapped princess. Dancers clad in colorful costumes perform intricate sword movements, symbolizing the epic struggle and eventual triumph of good over evil. This ancient dance is an unmissable spectacle and a testament to the island's traditional values.

B. Vela Gospa Pilgrimage:

Every year on August 15th, locals and visitors gather to celebrate the Assumption of the Virgin

Mary at the pilgrimage site of Vela Gospa. The island's religious fervor comes to life during this event, with processions, church services, and a sense of unity that highlights the island's tight-knit community.

III. Natural Beauty:

Korčula Island is a nature lover's paradise, boasting a diverse range of landscapes that captivate the senses.

A. Pristine Beaches:

The island is home to numerous beautiful beaches, each with its own unique charm. Vela Pržina in Lumbarda is a favorite for families, with its shallow waters and sandy shoreline. For those seeking tranquility, Pupnatska Luka's secluded bay provides a perfect escape. The clear waters and underwater biodiversity also make Korčula a haven for snorkeling and scuba diving enthusiasts.

B. Breathtaking Views:

The hilly terrain of the island offers breathtaking viewpoints, such as Sveti Ilija, where visitors can hike to witness panoramic vistas of the Adriatic Sea and nearby archipelago. The dense forests and vineyard-covered hills add to the island's beauty, making it a paradise for hikers and nature enthusiasts.

IV. Gastronomy:

No travel guide would be complete without exploring the local culinary delights, and Korčula Island does not disappoint.

A. Seafood Delicacies:

As an island surrounded by the Adriatic Sea, Korčula is a haven for seafood lovers. Restaurants and konobas (traditional Croatian taverns) offer delectable dishes like black risotto, made with squid ink, and freshly grilled fish caught by local fishermen.

B. Korčula Wines:

The island's fertile soil and favorable climate provide an ideal environment for vineyards. Grk, a unique indigenous white grape variety, is grown exclusively on the island and produces a refreshing and aromatic wine that pairs perfectly with local seafood.

V. Activities and Excursions:

Apart from its historical and cultural charm, Korčula Island offers a range of activities and excursions for an unforgettable experience.

A. Water Sports:

With its crystal-clear waters, Korčula is ideal for water sports such as kayaking, paddleboarding, and sailing. Numerous water sports centers offer equipment rentals and guided tours, catering to both beginners and experienced adventurers.

B. Island Hopping:

Using Korčula Town as a base, visitors can easily explore nearby islands like Mljet, Lastovo, and Hvar. Each island has its own distinctive character, landscapes, and attractions, making island hopping an enticing option.

Korčula Island in Croatia is a destination that captures the heart and soul of every traveler. Its unique blend of history, culture, natural beauty, and warm hospitality creates an unforgettable experience for those fortunate enough to visit. Whether you're strolling through the charming streets of Korčula Town, partaking in the ancient Moreska Sword Dance, or savoring the local seafood delicacies and wines, Korčula Island promises an enriching journey that will leave you with lasting memories. Embrace the allure of this Croatian gem, and let the magic of Korčula sweep you off your feet.

Marco Polo's Birthplace

Croatia, situated at the crossroads of Central and Southeast Europe, boasts a rich history and a diverse landscape that draws travelers from all over the world. One of Croatia's most fascinating historical figures is Marco Polo, the renowned Venetian merchant, explorer, and writer. While many may associate him with Venice, Italy, there is an ongoing debate among historians and scholars about his true birthplace. The claim that Marco Polo was born on the picturesque island of Korcula, Croatia, has gained substantial attention in recent years. In this Croatia travel guide, we delve into the intriguing story of Korcula Island, exploring its history, culture, and the connection to the legendary explorer Marco Polo.

1. The Enchanting Island of Korcula:

Korcula Island, located in the Adriatic Sea, is one of Croatia's most enchanting and historically significant islands. With a rugged coastline, lush greenery, and charming villages, Korcula offers visitors a captivating blend of natural beauty and cultural heritage. Its proximity to the mainland and other Croatian islands makes it easily accessible and a popular destination for both local and international travelers.

2. A Journey Through History:

To understand the significance of Marco Polo's potential birthplace on Korcula Island, it's essential to explore the island's rich history. The region has seen the rise and fall of numerous empires and civilizations, from the Greeks and Romans to the Venetians and the Austro-Hungarian Empire. Each conqueror left its mark on the island, contributing to its unique cultural tapestry.

3. The Marco Polo Controversy:
The question of Marco Polo's birthplace has long been a subject of debate. Traditionally, it was widely believed that Marco Polo was born in Venice, Italy, in 1254. However, Croatian historians and some contemporary scholars have put forward compelling arguments that suggest Korcula Island as his true birthplace. The evidence supporting this claim includes historical documents and local legends that link the Polo family to the island.

4. The Polo Family in Korcula:
According to some local legends, Marco Polo's family had ancestral ties to Korcula. The story goes that his father, Niccolo Polo, and uncle, Maffeo Polo, were merchants who frequently traded in the region and had close ties to the island's community. It is said that Niccolo met Marco's mother during his stay on the island, and Marco Polo was born on Korcula before his family moved to Venice. While these tales have been passed down through generations, they lack definitive evidence to confirm their authenticity.

5. Tracing Marco Polo's Footsteps:

For travelers interested in exploring the potential birthplace of Marco Polo, Korcula offers a few key locations associated with the Polo family. The first is the alleged birth house of Marco Polo, a modest stone building that stands in the old town of Korcula. While the authenticity of this claim is uncertain, the house serves as a fascinating historical site and a reminder of the island's connection to the famous explorer.

6. *The Enigmatic Old Town of Korcula:*
Korcula's old town is a well-preserved medieval gem, enclosed by ancient walls and fortified towers. Navigating through its narrow, winding streets, travelers are transported back in time. The architecture of the old town reflects various influences, including Venetian, Gothic, and Renaissance styles. Visitors can explore the St. Mark's Cathedral, the Arneri Palace, and the Town Museum to learn more about the island's intriguing past.

7. *Embracing Korcula's Culture:*
Croatia is known for its vibrant cultural scene, and Korcula is no exception. The island hosts numerous cultural events, including traditional festivals, art exhibitions, and music performances. The Moreska Sword Dance, a captivating traditional dance, is one such event that showcases Korcula's unique cultural heritage and medieval origins.

8. *Indulging in Gastronomic Delights:*

A trip to Croatia would not be complete without savoring its delectable cuisine. Korcula, as an island, boasts an abundance of fresh seafood, delicious olive oil, and local wines. The island's restaurants and taverns offer a delightful array of dishes, providing a true taste of the Adriatic.

9. *Exploring the Surrounding Beauty:*

While Marco Polo's potential birthplace is a major draw, Korcula Island has much more to offer. The island's natural beauty is best experienced by exploring its pristine beaches, scenic hiking trails, and charming vineyards. A boat trip to the nearby islets and caves, such as Badija and Vrnik, allows visitors to immerse themselves in the stunning landscapes of the Adriatic.

Korcula Island, Croatia, is a captivating destination with a rich history and a strong claim to being the birthplace of the legendary explorer, Marco Polo. Whether one is drawn to the island's historical significance, its picturesque landscapes, or its vibrant culture, Korcula offers a unique and unforgettable experience for travelers seeking to unravel the mysteries of the past while enjoying the beauty of the present. As the debate surrounding Marco Polo's birthplace continues, visitors can indulge in the island's charm and create their own unforgettable memories on this enchanting Croatian gem.

Wine Tasting and Beaches

Croatia, with its stunning Adriatic coastline and rich history, has become an increasingly popular travel destination. One of the jewels in Croatia's crown is the picturesque Korcula Island. Situated in the southern part of the country, Korcula Island is renowned for its captivating blend of pristine beaches and excellent wine culture. This Croatia travel guide will delve into the enchanting world of wine tasting and beaches on Korcula Island, exploring the island's unique offerings, wine-making traditions, and must-visit beaches.

Korcula Island - A Jewel in the Adriatic Sea
Korcula Island Overview
Korcula Island is a splendid combination of lush vegetation, idyllic bays, and crystal-clear waters. It is the sixth-largest island in the Adriatic Sea and boasts a rich history dating back to ancient times. The island's strategic location made it a crucial point in various civilizations, and remnants of its past can be seen in the charming medieval town of Korcula, known as "Little Dubrovnik."

Getting to Korcula Island
Korcula Island is accessible by ferry from multiple locations, including Split, Dubrovnik, and other nearby islands. The ferry ride itself offers breathtaking views of the Adriatic, adding to the overall experience of visiting this beautiful island.

Wine Tasting in Korcula Island

Korcula Island's Wine-Making Heritage

The wine-making tradition on Korcula Island dates back thousands of years. The island's favorable climate, with warm summers and mild winters, along with its rich soil, creates ideal conditions for grape cultivation. The locals take immense pride in their wine-making heritage, and the island is home to several family-run wineries, each producing unique and exceptional wines.

Notable Grape Varieties

The two most prominent grape varieties on Korcula Island are Grk and Posip. Grk is indigenous to the island and is used to produce a dry, aromatic white wine. Posip, on the other hand, is a robust and flavorful white grape variety, resulting in a full-bodied and fruity wine.

Wine Tasting Experiences

Tourists visiting Korcula Island have the opportunity to partake in delightful wine tasting experiences. Many wineries welcome visitors to their estates, providing insights into the wine-making process and allowing them to sample an array of wines. The warmth and hospitality of the local winemakers make these experiences all the more enjoyable.

The Enchanting Beaches of Korcula Island

Korcula Island's Beach Diversity

Korcula Island boasts an impressive array of beaches, ranging from secluded coves to long stretches of sandy shoreline. The clear turquoise waters of the Adriatic Sea make for a perfect setting to relax and unwind.

Vela Przina Beach
Located near the village of Lumbarda, Vela Przina Beach is one of the most popular and well-known beaches on Korcula Island. With its fine golden sand and shallow waters, it is ideal for families with children. The picturesque surroundings and gentle breeze add to the allure of this beach.

Pupnatska Luka
Pupnatska Luka is a hidden gem tucked away in a secluded bay on the southern coast of the island. Surrounded by cliffs and lush greenery, this pebble beach offers a more intimate and tranquil atmosphere for those seeking a peaceful retreat.

Proizd Island
For a truly unique beach experience, visitors can take a boat trip to Proizd Island, located just off the coast of Vela Luka. This small island is renowned for its stunning white pebble beach and crystal-clear waters, making it a haven for snorkelers and nature lovers.

Exploring Korcula Town and Beyond
Korcula Town - A Medieval Marvel

Korcula Town, situated on the northeastern tip of the island, is often referred to as a smaller version of Dubrovnik. Enclosed by fortified walls, the town exudes an old-world charm with its narrow streets, red-roofed houses, and historic buildings. Visitors can explore the iconic St. Mark's Cathedral and climb the Marco Polo Tower for panoramic views of the town and the surrounding sea.

Beyond Korcula Town
While Korcula Town is a highlight of the island, there is much more to explore. The picturesque villages scattered across the island offer a glimpse into the authentic Croatian way of life. The tranquil countryside, dotted with vineyards and olive groves, invites travelers to take leisurely strolls and immerse themselves in the island's natural beauty.

Korcula Island in Croatia is a perfect destination for travelers seeking a delightful blend of wine tasting and beach experiences. The island's rich wine-making heritage, with indigenous grape varieties, makes it a paradise for wine enthusiasts. Moreover, its diverse and beautiful beaches offer opportunities for relaxation and adventure alike. Whether you choose to explore the medieval town of Korcula or venture into the island's charming villages, Korcula promises a memorable and enchanting journey through Croatia's treasures on the Adriatic.

CHAPTER FIVE

Croatia's Culinary Delights

• *Traditional Dishes and Cuisine*

Croatia, a stunning country situated in the heart of Europe, boasts a diverse and delicious culinary heritage that reflects its unique history and geographical location. With a rich tapestry of influences from various cultures that have passed through the region over the centuries, Croatian cuisine offers an exquisite blend of flavors and ingredients. In this comprehensive travel guide, we will delve into the traditional dishes and cuisine of Croatia, exploring its regional specialties, culinary traditions, and must-visit restaurants and markets. From the Adriatic coastline to the lush inland regions, get ready to embark on a culinary journey like no other.

1. Historical and Geographical Influences on Croatian Cuisine:

Croatian cuisine has been shaped by a fascinating amalgamation of influences from the Mediterranean, Ottoman, Hungarian, and Austrian cultures. Being situated at the crossroads of Central and Southeast Europe, the country's cuisine is a reflection of its diverse history. The coastal regions are heavily influenced by Italian and Greek culinary traditions, while the inland areas incorporate elements of Central European and Balkan cuisine.

2. Coastal Delicacies:

a. Fresh Seafood and Adriatic Fish: Croatia's coastline stretches over 1,100 miles along the Adriatic Sea, making seafood an integral part of the coastal diet. Fish such as sea bass, grouper, and bream are commonly grilled or baked and served with olive oil, garlic, and aromatic herbs.

b. Black Risotto (Crni rižot): A unique dish hailing from the Dalmatian coast, black risotto gets its striking color from squid ink. Prepared with rice, cuttlefish or squid, garlic, wine, and fish broth, this dish is a delightful treat for seafood lovers.

c. Octopus Salad (Salata od hobotnice): This refreshing salad combines tender octopus, potatoes, onions, capers, and olive oil, often seasoned with parsley and lemon, showcasing the Mediterranean flavors at their finest.

3. Inland Treasures:

a. Peka: One of Croatia's most cherished dishes, peka is a slow-cooked delight prepared under a bell-like dome covered with embers. The dish usually consists of meat (lamb, veal, or chicken) and potatoes, seasoned with herbs and drizzled with olive oil.

b. Strukli: A delightful pastry from the northern regions, strukli is made from dough rolled thinly and filled with cottage cheese, sour cream, and eggs, creating a delectable blend of textures and flavors.

c. Čobanac: A hearty stew popular in Slavonia, Čobanac is prepared with mixed meats (often including beef, pork, and game), vegetables, and an array of spices, creating a robust and flavorful dish.

4. Unique Regional Specialties:

a. Istria: Known as the "Tuscany of Croatia," Istria offers dishes like fuži (handmade pasta) with truffles, maneštra (a vegetable and bean stew), and delicious local olive oils.

b. Dalmatia: This region is renowned for its aromatic herbs, which flavor dishes like pasticada (beef stew) and soparnik (a Swiss chard pie).

c. Zagorje: The hills of Zagorje are famous for dishes like zagorski štrukli (a rolled pastry filled with cottage cheese) and turkey with mlinci (thin, dried flatbread).

5. Unmissable Food Experiences:

a. Local Markets: To fully experience the essence of Croatian cuisine, visit the bustling local markets like Dolac in Zagreb or Split's Pazar. Here, you'll find fresh produce, cured meats, cheeses, and other traditional delicacies.

b. Olive Oil Tasting: Croatia is home to some of the world's finest olive oils, particularly those from Istria and Dalmatia. Participate in an olive oil tasting to savor the different varieties and learn about their production.

c. Wine Tours: Croatia's wine culture is thriving, with diverse regions producing excellent wines. Embark on a wine tour to taste indigenous varieties like Plavac Mali and Graševina while enjoying breathtaking landscapes.

6. Traditional Desserts:

a. Fritule: These small doughnut-like treats are popular during festivals and holidays. They are flavored with lemon zest, rum, and raisins, then dusted with powdered sugar.

b. Rozata: A Croatian version of crème caramel, rozata is a creamy custard infused with vanilla and citrus zest, typically served with caramel sauce.

c. Krafne: Croatian doughnuts, known as krafne, are filled with jam or chocolate and are an absolute delight to indulge in.

Croatian cuisine is a treasure trove of diverse flavors, history, and tradition. From the fresh seafood of the Adriatic coast to the hearty stews of the inland regions, each dish tells a story of Croatia's rich cultural heritage. Exploring the traditional dishes and cuisine of Croatia is an essential aspect of any visit to this beautiful country, as it provides a deeper understanding of its people and their way of life. Whether you're a seasoned foodie or a curious traveler, Croatia's culinary delights will leave you with an unforgettable experience that will linger on your taste buds and in your heart for years to come.

Popular Restaurants and Local Eateries

Croatia, a captivating country nestled along the Adriatic Sea, is a treasure trove of natural beauty and cultural wonders. As travelers explore its picturesque landscapes and historical sites, they also encounter an equally enticing culinary scene.

Croatia's cuisine is a delightful blend of Mediterranean, Balkan, and Central European influences, offering an array of mouthwatering dishes and flavors. In this comprehensive Croatia travel guide, we delve into the world of popular restaurants and local eateries, inviting food enthusiasts to embark on a gastronomic adventure through the country's diverse culinary landscape.

1. The Rich Culinary Heritage of Croatia:

Croatian cuisine is deeply rooted in tradition, and each region boasts its own unique culinary specialties. The coastal areas, such as Istria, Dalmatia, and Dubrovnik, celebrate seafood delicacies like grilled fish, octopus salad, and black risotto made with cuttlefish ink. Inland regions like Zagreb and Slavonia offer hearty dishes like strukli (pastry filled with cottage cheese), kulen (spicy sausage), and štrukli (pasta filled with cheese). Visitors can savor these regional delights at popular restaurants and local eateries throughout the country.

2. Must-Visit Restaurants in Zagreb:

As the vibrant capital city of Croatia, Zagreb boasts a thriving dining scene that caters to all tastes and budgets. For an upscale culinary experience, Trilogija offers a refined menu featuring modern Croatian cuisine with a touch of international flair. Those looking to indulge in traditional dishes can visit Vinodol, a beloved restaurant serving hearty stews, roasted meats, and delectable desserts. Adventurous foodies can explore the world of "štrukli" at La Štruk, where they can sample both sweet and savory variations of this iconic Croatian dish.

3. The Delights of Istria:

The picturesque Istrian peninsula is a food lover's paradise, renowned for its truffles, olive oil, and seafood. For a memorable dining experience, head to Batelina, a small family-run restaurant in Banjole, known for its innovative seafood creations. In Rovinj, Monte stands as a culinary gem with its unique fusion of Istrian and Mediterranean flavors. The city of Motovun is famous for its truffles, and visitors can indulge in these luxurious delights at restaurants like Konoba Mondo and Zigante Tartufi.

4. Exploring Dalmatian Cuisine:

Dalmatia, with its stunning coastline and historical towns, is equally captivating in its culinary offerings. In Split, travelers can enjoy fresh seafood at Apetit, a restaurant that blends tradition with modern culinary techniques. Pelegrini, located in Šibenik, showcases a refined take on Dalmatian cuisine and has been awarded a Michelin star for its exceptional dishes. For a more casual experience, try konobas (taverns) like Konoba Nikola in Hvar or

Konoba Mate in Korčula, where you can savor authentic Dalmatian recipes passed down through generations.

5. The Enchanting Flavors of Dubrovnik:

Dubrovnik, known as the "Pearl of the Adriatic," offers an enchanting mix of historical charm and delectable cuisine. Nautika, set against the backdrop of Dubrovnik's ancient walls, offers a luxurious dining experience featuring fresh seafood and Croatian wines. To sample traditional dishes in a cozy setting, visit Konoba Pupo, where you can try local specialties like "Zelena Menestra" (green stew) and "Rozata" (custard dessert).

6. Charming Local Eateries Off the Beaten Path:

While popular restaurants offer an exquisite dining experience, some of the most memorable meals can be found in small local eateries hidden in Croatia's charming towns and villages. In the heart of the Pelješac peninsula, visit Konoba Skojera in Žuljana, a rustic tavern known for its homemade seafood dishes and warm hospitality. On the island of Vis, Bistro po Kavama captivates visitors with its simple yet delicious dishes, made from fresh local ingredients.

7. Embracing the Wine Culture:

Croatia's diverse landscape also gives rise to excellent wine regions, such as Istria, Pelješac, and the Dalmatian coast. Don't miss the opportunity to pair your meals with renowned Croatian wines, including Malvasia, Plavac Mali, and Pošip. Many local eateries feature an extensive wine list, allowing travelers to indulge in the country's rich wine culture.

Embarking on a culinary journey through Croatia is a delightful experience that immerses travelers in the country's rich history, vibrant culture, and delectable flavors. From popular restaurants in bustling cities to charming local eateries hidden in idyllic villages, Croatia offers an enticing array of dishes that celebrate its diverse culinary heritage. Whether indulging in fresh seafood along the coast or savoring hearty stews in the inland regions, visitors are sure to be captivated by the authentic tastes and warm hospitality that define Croatian cuisine. So, pack your bags, prepare your taste buds, and let Croatia's gastronomic wonders take you on an unforgettable adventure.

•*Wine Regions and Tastings*

Croatia, a stunning gem in Southeast Europe, is renowned for its breathtaking landscapes, rich history, and diverse culture. But beyond its historical treasures and coastal beauty, Croatia has also emerged as a prominent wine-producing country. From the sun-soaked vineyards to the traditional wine cellars, Croatia offers a unique and enriching wine-tasting experience for enthusiasts and novices alike. In this travel guide, we will explore the fascinating wine regions of Croatia, delve into the country's winemaking history, and uncover the must-visit wineries for an unforgettable wine-tasting adventure.

1. Croatia's Winemaking Heritage

Croatia boasts a long and storied history of winemaking that dates back thousands of years. The ancient Greeks introduced viticulture to the region, and throughout the centuries, various civilizations, including the Romans and Illyrians, further nurtured the tradition of winemaking. The country's diverse climate and geographical features have led to the cultivation of numerous grape varieties, some of which are indigenous to Croatia.

2. Wine Regions of Croatia

2.1 Istria

Located in the northwest of Croatia, Istria is one of the country's most prominent wine regions. Blessed with a Mediterranean climate, the region's rolling hills and fertile soil provide ideal conditions for growing several grape varieties, including Malvazija Istriana and Teran. Visitors can explore charming family-run wineries, where they can savor some of Istria's top-quality wines while enjoying the scenic beauty of the countryside.

2.2 Dalmatia

Dalmatia, situated along the stunning Adriatic coast, is another significant wine-producing region in Croatia. This area is famous for producing the robust red wine Plavac Mali, as well as the popular white wine varieties such as Pošip and Maraština. The coastal breeze and ample sunshine contribute to the unique character of Dalmatian wines, making it a must-visit destination for wine lovers.

2.3 Slavonia

Moving towards the eastern part of Croatia, we find the region of Slavonia. Known for its vast vineyards and picturesque landscapes, Slavonia offers a different winemaking experience. The region primarily focuses on white wine varieties, with Graševina being the most celebrated one. Visitors can explore traditional wine cellars known as "podrumi" and witness the winemaking process, which is often done with great reverence to age-old customs.

2.4 Kvarner

Kvarner, with its unique blend of mountainous terrains and coastal charm, is an emerging wine region in Croatia. This area produces a variety of wines, including some outstanding Chardonnays and Zlahtina. The scenic beauty of Kvarner, combined with its growing reputation in the wine world, makes it a hidden gem for wine enthusiasts to explore.

3. Wine Tasting Experiences

3.1 Winery Tours

Visiting wineries is the most immersive way to experience Croatian wines. Many wineries offer guided tours where visitors can learn about the winemaking process, history, and unique characteristics of each wine. Some wineries also provide the opportunity to participate in grape harvesting and traditional wine-making activities.

3.2 Wine Festivals

Throughout the year, Croatia hosts several wine festivals celebrating regional wines. One of the most popular is the Vinistra festival in Istria, where wine enthusiasts and producers gather to showcase their finest wines. These festivals offer a vibrant atmosphere, cultural performances, and, of course, the chance to taste an extensive array of wines.

3.3 Wine Bars and Restaurants

Croatia's cities and towns are home to charming wine bars and restaurants that offer an extensive selection of local wines. These establishments often have sommeliers who can guide you through the wine list and recommend pairings with delicious Croatian cuisine.

4. Notable Wineries in Croatia

4.1 Korta Katarina Winery, Pelješac Peninsula

Korta Katarina is a renowned winery located in the picturesque Pelješac Peninsula. Their award-winning Plavac Mali and Pošip wines have garnered international recognition. The winery also offers luxurious accommodation and a stunning view of the Adriatic Sea.

4.2 Roxanich Winery, Istria

Roxanich Winery is famous for its dedication to organic and biodynamic winemaking practices. Their artisanal approach has resulted in exceptional wines that showcase the uniqueness of Istria's terroir.

4.3 Krauthaker Winery, Slavonia

Situated in the heart of Slavonia, Krauthaker Winery is known for producing top-quality Graševina wines. The winery's welcoming ambiance and warm hospitality make it a must-visit destination for wine enthusiasts.

Croatia's wine regions offer a delightful blend of history, culture, and unparalleled wine-tasting experiences. From the sun-kissed vineyards of Istria to the traditional wine cellars of Slavonia, each region has a unique story to tell through its wines. Whether you are a seasoned wine connoisseur or someone looking to embark on a wine-tasting adventure, Croatia promises to be a memorable and enriching destination for wine lovers. So raise your glass and toast to the charm of Croatian wines, and let the journey of discovery begin in this enchanting land.

CHAPTER SIX

Outdoor Activities and Adventures

• *Sailing the Adriatic Coast*

Croatia, a breathtaking Mediterranean country known for its stunning coastline, crystal-clear waters, and rich history, offers an unforgettable sailing experience along the Adriatic Coast. With more than a thousand islands and islets scattered along the coast, sailing in Croatia promises a diverse and captivating journey. This travel guide aims to provide you with a comprehensive overview of sailing in Croatia, covering everything from planning your trip to exploring the enchanting destinations along the Adriatic Coast.

1. Why Choose Sailing in Croatia:

Croatia has earned a reputation as one of the world's top sailing destinations for several reasons. The Adriatic Sea's calm waters, numerous sheltered bays, and well-developed marinas make it an ideal spot for both experienced sailors and beginners alike. The combination of the country's natural beauty, cultural heritage, and excellent sailing infrastructure creates a unique and unforgettable sailing experience.

2. *Planning Your Sailing Trip:*

a. Best Time to Sail:
The sailing season in Croatia typically runs from May to October, with July and August being the peak months. During these months, the weather is warm and sunny, and the sea is calm, providing ideal conditions for sailing. However, if you prefer a quieter and less crowded experience, consider sailing during the shoulder seasons of May-June and September-October.

b. Choosing a Yacht:
When selecting a yacht for your sailing adventure, you have various options, including bareboat charters, crewed charters, and flotilla sailing. If you have sailing experience and the necessary licenses, you can opt for a bareboat charter, giving you the freedom to navigate the waters independently. For a more luxurious experience, a crewed charter allows you to relax as a professional crew takes care of everything. Flotilla sailing offers a perfect balance by providing the freedom of bareboat charters with the support of a flotilla lead boat.

c. Sailing Itinerary:
Create a flexible sailing itinerary to explore Croatia's diverse coastal regions and islands. Popular starting points include Split, Zadar, and

Dubrovnik. Depending on your preferences and the duration of your trip, plan visits to islands like Hvar, Vis, Korčula, Brač, and the Kornati National Park. Each island has its unique charm, from vibrant nightlife to secluded beaches and ancient towns.

3. Navigating the Adriatic Coast:

a. Sailing Regulations:
Before embarking on your sailing adventure, familiarize yourself with Croatia's sailing regulations. Ensure you have all the required documents, including your sailing license, passport, and boat papers. Familiarize yourself with the local maritime rules and regulations, such as speed limits, anchoring guidelines, and protected marine areas.

b. Weather and Sea Conditions:
While the Adriatic Sea is generally calm and safe for sailing, it's essential to stay informed about weather forecasts and potential changes in sea conditions. Sudden Bora and Jugo winds can occur, particularly in the spring and fall, so having a basic understanding of weather patterns is crucial for a safe journey.

c. Mooring and Marinas:
Croatia boasts a well-developed network of marinas and harbors along the coast and on the islands. It's advisable to make reservations in advance during

the peak season to secure your spot. Additionally, many islands offer the opportunity to moor in secluded coves or anchor in pristine bays, providing a more serene experience.

4. Sailing Destinations along the Adriatic Coast:

a. Split:
Split, the second-largest city in Croatia, is a popular starting point for many sailing routes. Explore the historic Diocletian's Palace, a UNESCO World Heritage Site, and experience the vibrant local culture in the city's narrow streets and bustling markets.

b. Hvar:
Known for its vibrant nightlife and stunning beaches, Hvar is a must-visit island. Enjoy the chic restaurants, bars, and clubs, and don't miss the opportunity to witness the mesmerizing sunset from the fortress above the town.

c. Vis:
Vis offers a more tranquil atmosphere compared to some of the more party-centric islands. Explore its untouched beauty, hidden coves, and stunning Blue Cave, a natural wonder that illuminates the water with a mesmerizing blue hue.

d. Korčula:

Rich in history and folklore, Korčula is believed to be the birthplace of the famous explorer Marco Polo. Wander through the enchanting medieval streets and enjoy the island's picturesque landscapes.

e. Kornati National Park:
A true paradise for nature lovers, the Kornati National Park consists of 89 uninhabited islands, islets, and reefs. The raw beauty of the islands and the clear waters make it a perfect spot for diving and snorkeling.

5. *Embracing Croatian Culture and Cuisine:*

While sailing the Adriatic Coast, you'll have the opportunity to immerse yourself in the rich Croatian culture and savor its delicious cuisine. Visit local markets to sample fresh seafood, olive oil, cheese, and wine. Engage with the friendly locals and learn about their traditions, history, and way of life.

Sailing the Adriatic Coast in Croatia is an unparalleled experience that combines natural beauty, rich history, and diverse island landscapes. Whether you're an experienced sailor or a first-time adventurer, Croatia's welcoming waters and picturesque islands offer an unforgettable journey. Plan your trip carefully, embrace the local culture, and embark on a sailing adventure that will create lasting memories for a lifetime. So, set sail and let the wonders of Croatia's coast enchant you as you explore the treasures of the Adriatic Sea.

•Hiking and Trekking Trails

Nestled in the heart of Europe, Croatia is a country that boasts an abundance of natural beauty and diverse landscapes, making it an ideal destination for hikers and trekkers alike. With its picturesque coastline along the Adriatic Sea, lush green national parks, rugged mountains, and charming rural villages, Croatia offers a plethora of hiking and trekking trails for outdoor enthusiasts. This comprehensive travel guide will delve into the best hiking and trekking trails across the country, covering its unique geography, popular destinations, safety tips, and the best times to embark on these adventures.

1. Croatia's Diverse Geography:

Croatia's diverse geography creates a tapestry of scenic trails catering to all levels of hikers and trekkers. The country can be roughly divided into three regions:

A. Coastal Region: Croatia's stunning coastline stretches for over 1,100 miles, dotted with picturesque islands, hidden coves, and charming towns. The coastal region offers a mix of leisurely seaside strolls and more challenging hikes along cliffs and hills.

B. Inland Region: The inland area is characterized by rolling hills, lush valleys, and captivating forests. This region is home to several national parks, which provide some of the most rewarding trekking experiences.

C. Mountainous Region: The Dinaric Alps dominate Croatia's eastern border, offering rugged peaks, dramatic gorges, and a variety of trails catering to experienced hikers and adventurers.

2. *Popular Hiking and Trekking Destinations:*

A. Plitvice Lakes National Park: One of Croatia's most famous natural wonders, Plitvice Lakes National Park features a series of interconnected lakes, cascading waterfalls, and wooden walkways that allow visitors to explore this UNESCO World Heritage site. The park offers various hiking trails ranging from easy strolls to longer treks, providing breathtaking views of its crystal-clear lakes and diverse wildlife.

B. Paklenica National Park: Situated at the southern edge of the Velebit mountain range, Paklenica National Park offers an array of challenging treks through karst landscapes, dense forests, and impressive canyons. The park is a paradise for rock climbers as well, with its imposing cliffs attracting enthusiasts from all over the world.

C. Mljet National Park: The island of Mljet, located in the Adriatic Sea, is home to Croatia's only national park situated on an island. With its lush vegetation, saltwater lakes, and ancient ruins, Mljet provides a unique hiking experience in a serene and pristine environment.

D. Mount Biokovo: Rising majestically above the Adriatic coast, Mount Biokovo offers breathtaking panoramic views of the sea and the islands below. There are several well-marked trails, and reaching the highest peak, Sveti Jure, rewards hikers with an unforgettable experience.

E. Hvar Island: Known for its vibrant nightlife and stunning beaches, Hvar Island also hides a network of hiking trails that wind through lavender fields, olive groves, and charming villages. Hvar's diverse landscapes make it a captivating destination for hikers seeking a mix of culture and nature.

3. Best Times for Hiking and Trekking:

Croatia's climate offers distinct seasons, each providing a different experience for hikers and trekkers. The best times to explore the trails depend on personal preferences and the region being visited.

A. Spring (April to June): Spring is a delightful time to hike in Croatia, with blooming flowers, pleasant temperatures, and fewer tourists. The landscapes are lush and green, making it ideal for those seeking scenic beauty.

B. Summer (July to August): While summers can be hot and crowded, they are a great time to explore the coastal trails and enjoy the turquoise waters. Hiking in the mountainous regions might be challenging due to high temperatures, so it's advisable to hike early in the morning or late in the afternoon.

C. Autumn (September to October): Autumn brings milder temperatures and fewer crowds, making it an excellent time to explore both the coast and the national parks. The changing colors of the leaves add a touch of magic to the landscapes.

D. Winter (November to March): Winter is a quieter time in terms of tourism, and while some coastal hikes are still enjoyable, the mountainous trails might be covered in snow and pose additional challenges.

4. Safety Tips for Hiking and Trekking:

As with any outdoor activity, safety should always be a priority. Here are some essential tips for a safe and enjoyable hiking or trekking experience in Croatia:

A. Plan Ahead: Research the trails you intend to explore, familiarize yourself with the route, and assess your fitness level to choose trails suitable for your abilities.

B. Wear Appropriate Gear: Invest in sturdy and comfortable hiking boots, breathable clothing, a hat, sunglasses, and sunscreen. Pack a waterproof jacket, plenty of water, snacks, a map, and a first aid kit.

C. Respect Nature: Croatia's natural beauty must be preserved. Stay on marked trails, avoid littering, and refrain from disturbing wildlife. Respect any guidelines and regulations set by park authorities.

D. Check Weather Conditions: Weather in Croatia can change quickly, especially in mountainous regions. Check the forecast before embarking on your hike and be prepared for unexpected changes.

E. Inform Someone: Before setting off on a hike or trek, inform a friend or family member about your plans, including your intended route and estimated return time.

Croatia's hiking and trekking trails offer a captivating blend of natural wonders, cultural experiences, and unforgettable adventures. From the awe-inspiring waterfalls of Plitvice Lakes to the rugged peaks of the Dinaric Alps, Croatia caters to hikers and trekkers of all levels, providing an opportunity to immerse themselves in the country's breathtaking landscapes and rich heritage. Whether you seek a leisurely coastal stroll or a challenging mountain trek, Croatia's diverse geography promises an unforgettable journey for every outdoor enthusiast. So, pack your hiking gear, embrace the spirit of exploration, and embark on an unforgettable adventure through Croatia's enchanting trails.

•*Water Sports and Diving*

Croatia, a captivating country located on the Adriatic Sea, is a haven for water enthusiasts and adventure seekers. With its pristine coastlines, crystal-clear waters, and numerous islands, Croatia offers a plethora of water sports and diving opportunities. From thrilling adrenaline-pumping activities to serene underwater explorations, the country has something to cater to every water lover's dream. This comprehensive travel guide will take you on a journey through Croatia's top water sports and diving destinations, providing essential information, safety tips, and recommendations to ensure a memorable aquatic adventure.

I. Croatia's Coastal Beauty:

Before diving into the world of water sports and diving, it's essential to appreciate Croatia's breathtaking coastal beauty. With over a thousand islands scattered along the coast, Croatia's azure waters and stunning landscapes create an idyllic backdrop for aquatic activities. The Dalmatian Coast, Istria, and Kvarner are some of the most popular regions that boast not only fantastic water sports opportunities but also historical sites, picturesque towns, and delicious cuisine.

II. Top Water Sports in Croatia:

1. Windsurfing and Kitesurfing:

Croatia's consistent winds and well-suited coastal geography make it a prime destination for windsurfing and kitesurfing. Viganj, Bol, and Premantura are among the best spots for these adrenaline-fueled sports, offering rental services, lessons, and ideal conditions for both beginners and experienced enthusiasts.

2. Jet Skiing:

For those seeking fast-paced excitement, jet skiing is a favorite activity along the Croatian coast. Split, Hvar, and Zrće Beach on Pag Island are known for their jet ski rentals and designated areas for thrilling rides.

3. Sailing and Yachting:

Sailing and yachting enthusiasts will find their paradise in Croatia. With its myriad of islands and secluded coves, sailing along the Adriatic offers a unique perspective of the country's natural beauty. Charter services are readily available, and marinas are well-equipped to accommodate boaters of all levels.

4. Kayaking and Paddleboarding:

Exploring Croatia's hidden bays and sea caves by kayak or paddleboard is a serene and intimate experience. The Pakleni Islands, Elafiti Islands, and the Plitvice Lakes National Park are some of the top spots for these water sports, providing a chance to witness Croatia's untouched nature up close.

III. Diving in Croatia:

1. Underwater Paradises:

Croatia's underwater world is a hidden treasure trove waiting to be explored. The Adriatic Sea's clear visibility and diverse marine life make it an alluring destination for scuba divers. The Kornati National Park, Vis Island, and the Brijuni Islands are renowned for their underwater beauty and protected marine areas.

2. Wreck Diving:

History enthusiasts and experienced divers can indulge in Croatia's rich history through wreck diving. The Adriatic houses numerous shipwrecks, some dating back to ancient times, while others are from more recent centuries. The Vis Island, with its famous "Brioni" shipwreck, is a popular destination for wreck diving.

3. Cave Diving:

For the daring and experienced, cave diving offers an unparalleled adventure. Croatia's underwater cave systems, such as the Blue Grotto on Biševo Island and the Modra Špilja on Vis Island, provide a unique challenge and an opportunity to explore nature's subterranean wonders.

IV. Safety Precautions and Conservation:

While indulging in water sports and diving, safety should always be a top priority. It's essential to respect the sea and its ecosystems to preserve them for future generations. This section of the guide will highlight important safety measures and promote responsible diving practices, including tips for protecting marine life and minimizing environmental impact.

V. Best Time to Visit for Water Sports and Diving:

Croatia's climate and water conditions vary throughout the year, influencing the best time to visit for specific water activities. This section will provide an overview of the country's climate, water temperatures, and peak seasons for each water sport and diving experience.

VI. Water Sports Events and Festivals:

Croatia's vibrant water sports community hosts various events and festivals throughout the year. From windsurfing competitions to sailing regattas, this section will introduce readers to some of the most exciting water sports gatherings in Croatia.

Croatia's aquatic allure extends far beyond its picturesque coastlines and idyllic islands. With a plethora of water sports and diving opportunities, the country invites travelers to explore its vibrant underwater world and partake in thrilling aquatic adventures. From the adrenaline rush of windsurfing to the tranquility of cave diving, Croatia offers a diverse range of activities for all types of water enthusiasts. As you embark on your aquatic journey, remember to prioritize safety, practice responsible diving, and immerse yourself in the wonders of Croatia's aquatic paradise. So pack your bags, grab your gear, and get ready to dive into the aquatic adventure of a lifetime in Croatia.

CHAPTER SEVEN

Cultural Experiences and Festivals

• *Croatian Folklore and Traditions*

Nestled at the crossroads of Central Europe, the Balkans, and the Mediterranean, Croatia is a land that boasts a diverse and captivating cultural heritage. One of the most intriguing aspects of Croatian culture is its folklore and traditions, which provide a unique insight into the country's history, customs, and way of life. This travel guide aims to delve deep into the colorful world of Croatian folklore and traditions, taking you on a journey through centuries of customs, rituals, music, dance, and culinary delights that continue to shape the nation's identity to this day.

1. Historical Background

Croatia's folklore and traditions can be traced back to ancient times when various tribes and cultures settled in the region. The early inhabitants, such as the Illyrians and the Romans, left their mark on Croatian culture, laying the foundation for the rich tapestry of traditions that exist today. Over the centuries, Croatia experienced the influences of the Byzantine Empire, the Ottoman Empire, and the Austro-Hungarian Empire, all of which contributed to the eclectic mix of customs and beliefs found within Croatian folklore.

2. Traditional Music and Dance

Music and dance hold a special place in Croatian folklore, acting as a bridge between the past and the present. The traditional music of Croatia varies from region to region, with distinct styles and instruments adding to the country's cultural diversity. Popular musical instruments include the tamburica, a stringed instrument similar to a mandolin, and the gusle, a single-stringed instrument played with a bow, often used in epic poetry performances.

Klapa singing, a form of acapella vocal music, is a cherished tradition in coastal areas like Dalmatia. UNESCO has recognized this unique form of singing as an intangible cultural heritage of humanity. Similarly, traditional dances like the Linđo, a lively dance from Dubrovnik, and the Kolo, a circle dance popular in Slavonia, continue to be celebrated at various festivals and events throughout the country.

3. Festivals and Celebrations

Croatia's calendar is brimming with festivals and celebrations, each reflecting the distinct character of the region in which they are held. One of the most famous events is the Dubrovnik Summer Festival, held annually since 1950. The festival showcases various artistic performances, including theater, music, and dance, against the stunning backdrop of Dubrovnik's historic walls.

In Istria, the region's rich agricultural heritage is celebrated with numerous truffle festivals, where visitors can indulge in the unique flavors of this prized delicacy. Other events, such as the Sinjska Alka in Sinj and the Rijeka Carnival, offer a glimpse into Croatia's martial traditions and exuberant carnival culture, respectively.

4. Traditional Clothing and Crafts

Traditional clothing, known as "narodna nošnja," plays a vital role in preserving Croatian heritage. Each region has its own distinctive style of clothing, often characterized by intricate embroidery, vibrant colors, and handwoven fabrics. The traditional clothing is still worn on special occasions and during folklore performances, allowing visitors to witness the living legacy of Croatian craftsmanship.

Croatia is also renowned for its traditional crafts, including pottery, lace-making, and filigree jewelry. The town of Samobor, for instance, is famous for its intricate gingerbread hearts, which are given as symbols of affection and good luck.

5. Customs and Superstitions

Croatian folklore is replete with customs and superstitions that have been passed down through generations. One such tradition is the welcoming of the new year, where locals perform the "Vasilica" ritual, lighting a bonfire and jumping over it to bring good luck and ward off evil spirits.

Additionally, there are numerous beliefs related to the supernatural world, with certain plants and animals considered to possess protective or healing properties. For instance, the olive tree is revered for its symbolic association with peace, while the red carnation is believed to bring good fortune.

6. Culinary Traditions

Croatian cuisine is an essential part of the country's folklore and traditions, showcasing a delightful blend of Mediterranean and Central European influences. Each region boasts its own culinary specialties, with seafood dominating the coastal areas, hearty stews in the continental regions, and delectable pastries and sweets throughout the country.

Traditional dishes such as "Peka," a slow-cooked meat and vegetable dish prepared under a metal lid, and "Ispod peke," where food is cooked under hot ashes, offer a glimpse into ancient cooking techniques still cherished by Croatians today. Not to be missed are the world-renowned Croatian wines, which have gained international recognition for their quality and distinct taste.

7. *Religious Customs*

Religion has played a significant role in shaping Croatian traditions and customs. The majority of Croatians identify as Roman Catholics, and religious festivities are an essential part of the cultural calendar. Easter and Christmas are celebrated with great fervor, with various processions, ceremonies, and festive meals bringing families and communities together.

Croatia's folklore and traditions provide a fascinating lens through which to explore the country's cultural heritage. From traditional music and dance to vibrant festivals and customs, the nation's rich history comes alive through these enduring practices. As a traveler, immersing yourself in Croatian folklore allows you to connect with the heart and soul of the nation, forging unforgettable memories and gaining a deeper appreciation for the diversity and richness of Croatian culture. So, embark on a journey of discovery and let the enchanting world of Croatian folklore captivate your senses as you explore this mesmerizing land at the crossroads of history and tradition.

• *Music and Dance Festivals*

Croatia, a stunning Mediterranean country boasting pristine beaches, historic cities, and breathtaking landscapes, has emerged as a haven for music and dance enthusiasts. The country's vibrant cultural scene is exemplified by its numerous music and dance festivals, drawing revelers from all corners of the globe. This travel guide dives deep into Croatia's music and dance festival scene, offering a comprehensive overview of the most popular festivals, their unique features, and the experiences they promise to deliver.

1. *Croatia's Festival Culture:*

Croatia's rich history and diverse heritage have significantly influenced its contemporary festival culture. Traditional festivals often incorporated music, dance, and various rituals, which have evolved into the modern-day extravaganzas that enthrall thousands of festival-goers. Festivals in Croatia have become a symbol of unity, celebration, and the joy of life, making them an integral part of the country's identity.

2. *A Sea of Festivals: An Overview*

Croatia hosts an impressive array of music and dance festivals throughout the year, catering to different tastes and preferences. Some of the most renowned festivals include:

a. Ultra Europe:
- Location: Split
- Description: As part of the globally acclaimed Ultra Music Festival brand, Ultra Europe brings together some of the biggest names in electronic dance music (EDM) to the stunning Dalmatian coast. The festival spans several days and includes mesmerizing light shows and electrifying performances.

b. INmusic Festival:
- Location: Zagreb
- Description: Nestled on the picturesque Lake Jarun, INmusic Festival is one of the country's largest open-air festivals. This event attracts alternative and indie music enthusiasts, featuring a diverse lineup of international and local artists.

c. Dimensions Festival:
- Location: Pula
- Description: For electronic music aficionados, Dimensions Festival is a pilgrimage. Held in the awe-inspiring Pula Arena, an ancient Roman amphitheater, the festival creates a unique ambiance that blends history with contemporary beats.

d. Outlook Festival:
- Location: Pula
- Description: Another gem in Pula, Outlook Festival caters to lovers of bass-heavy sounds, including dubstep, reggae, and drum and bass. Set against the backdrop of Fort Punta Christo, the festival offers a captivating experience.

e. Electric Elephant:
- Location: Tisno
- Description: An intimate affair, Electric Elephant is set along the Adriatic Sea and offers a laid-back atmosphere perfect for those seeking a more relaxed festival experience.

3. Unique Festival Experiences:

Croatia's music and dance festivals offer much more than just a stage and speakers. The country's stunning natural beauty and diverse historical sites enhance the festival experience, making it truly unforgettable.

a. Island Festivals:
- Location: Various Croatian islands (e.g., Pag, Hvar)
- Description: Many festivals take place on Croatia's stunning islands, providing an idyllic setting with crystal-clear waters and sandy beaches. These island festivals offer a unique opportunity to enjoy music and dance while basking in the Mediterranean sun.

b. Boat Parties:
- Description: Some festivals incorporate boat parties into their itinerary, taking revelers on a cruise along the beautiful coastline. These boat parties feature music, dancing, and breathtaking views of the Adriatic Sea.

c. Festival After-Parties:
- Description: Croatia's festival scene doesn't end when the main stages close. After-parties are a prevalent feature, offering attendees the chance to continue the festivities in intimate club settings or exclusive beachside venues.

4. Tips for Festival-Goers:

a. Ticket and Accommodation:
- Buying festival tickets well in advance is essential, as popular events often sell out quickly. Additionally, securing accommodation early is crucial, as nearby hotels and hostels fill up fast.

b. Dressing Smartly:
- Croatia's festival season typically falls during the summer months, so lightweight and breathable clothing are recommended. Don't forget sunscreen and a hat to protect yourself from the sun.

c. Hydration and Snacks:
- Dancing and partying can be energy-draining, so staying hydrated is essential. Many festivals provide

free water stations, but it's always wise to bring a reusable water bottle. Packing some snacks can also help keep your energy levels up.

d. Embrace the Local Cuisine:
- Croatian cuisine offers a delightful array of dishes. Don't miss the opportunity to try local specialties and seafood delicacies during your festival adventures.

Croatia's music and dance festivals offer an unrivaled experience, combining world-class artists, picturesque locations, and a vibrant atmosphere. Whether you're a dedicated electronic music fan, an indie enthusiast, or simply seeking an unforgettable summer adventure, Croatia's festival scene has something to offer. Embrace the magic of these events, explore the country's diverse landscape, and immerse yourself in the joyous celebration of music and dance that Croatia has become known for.

• *Carnival Celebrations*

Croatia, a country nestled along the beautiful Adriatic coast, is renowned for its stunning landscapes, rich history, and diverse culture. One of the most captivating cultural events that have been celebrated for centuries is the Croatian Carnival, locally known as "Karneval" or "Maškare." This annual festivity is a time when the entire country comes alive with colorful parades, lively music, and vibrant costumes, as locals and visitors alike join together to revel in the joyful spirit of the carnival. In this Croatia travel guide, we will delve into the enchanting world of Croatian Carnival celebrations, exploring their origins, regional variations, and must-visit locations to experience this unique tradition.

1. Historical Origins of Carnival Celebrations in Croatia

The roots of Carnival celebrations in Croatia can be traced back to ancient times when pagan rituals marked the transition from winter to spring. Over the centuries, the tradition evolved, absorbing influences from different cultures, including Roman, Byzantine, and Venetian. In fact, Croatia's association with Venice during its history has significantly influenced the modern form of the Carnival celebrated today.

2. Seasonal Timing and Duration

The Carnival season in Croatia officially begins on January 6th, also known as Epiphany or the Feast of the Three Kings, and culminates on Shrove Tuesday, which falls 40 days before Easter. The period between these dates is a time of jubilation, marked by numerous festivities and events throughout the country.

3. Regional Variations in Carnival Celebrations

Croatia's diverse regions boast unique customs and traditions, and the Carnival celebrations are no exception. While some elements of the festivities are common across the country, certain regions have distinctive practices that make their Carnival celebrations truly special.

- Rijeka: Known as the Carnival capital of Croatia, Rijeka hosts one of the most extravagant and dynamic Carnival events in Europe. The Rijeka Carnival, dating back to the 19th century, features massive parades with elaborate floats, lively music, and masked participants from various carnival groups, called "Kasperi." The most iconic figure of the Rijeka Carnival is "Zvončari," who wear traditional sheepskin coats and large bells around their waist, believed to ward off evil spirits.

- Dubrovnik: In the coastal city of Dubrovnik, the Carnival tradition is called "Festa." The main event is the "Lazareti Parade," where masked participants gather in the historic Lazareti complex to showcase their creative costumes and celebrate in the old town's narrow streets.

- Šibenik: The Šibenik region's Carnival celebrations are characterized by the unique "Kurentovanje" ritual, inspired by the neighboring Slovenian tradition. During this event, participants dress as "Kurents," donning large sheepskin costumes and massive cowbells, believed to chase away winter and evil spirits.

4. Key Events and Activities during the Carnival Season

a) Opening Ceremony: The Carnival season commences with a grand opening ceremony, featuring a symbolic event such as the "release of the keys" to the city, signifying the temporary rule of the Carnival Prince and Princess.

b) Masked Balls: Throughout the Carnival season, various towns and cities organize glamorous masked balls where locals and visitors can showcase their creativity and don their most imaginative costumes.

c) Parades and Floats: Spectacular parades take place across Croatia, with intricately designed floats, traditional folk music, and exuberant dancers filling the streets with energy and merriment.

d) Competitions and Contests: Carnival-goers can participate in competitions for the best costumes, mask designs, and humorous performances, adding an element of friendly rivalry to the festivities.

e) Traditional Cuisine: Carnival season is an opportunity to indulge in a range of delicious treats, including fritule (small donut-like pastries), krafne (Croatian donuts), and various regional specialties.

5. Carnival Traditions and Symbolism

Croatian Carnival celebrations are deeply rooted in symbolism and tradition. The act of wearing masks and disguises during the festivities serves as a way to shed one's identity temporarily, allowing individuals to engage freely in merriment without fear of judgment. Symbolically, the masks also represent the blurring of societal hierarchies, enabling people from all walks of life to participate in the revelry as equals.

6. Carnival and Croatian Identity

Croatian Carnival celebrations play a crucial role in preserving and celebrating the country's cultural heritage. The festivities bring communities together, fostering a strong sense of camaraderie and pride in Croatian traditions. Moreover, they serve as a reminder of the nation's resilience in the face of historical challenges, where the spirit of celebration endured despite various hardships.

Croatia's Carnival celebrations are a captivating blend of ancient customs, regional variations, and contemporary revelry. The festivities offer a unique opportunity for travelers to immerse themselves in the vibrant culture of this beautiful country while creating unforgettable memories of joy and camaraderie. Whether it's joining the lively parades in Rijeka, admiring the creative costumes in Dubrovnik, or experiencing the distinctive Kurentovanje ritual in Šibenik, participating in the Croatian Carnival is an experience like no other. As you plan your journey to Croatia, make sure to time your visit to coincide with this enchanting tradition, for it promises an unforgettable and colorful celebration of Croatian identity and heritage.

CHAPTER EIGHT

Practical Tips for Travelers

• *Language and Communication*

Croatia, nestled in the heart of Europe along the Adriatic Sea, is a captivating destination that boasts a rich cultural heritage and stunning natural landscapes. As a traveler exploring this enchanting country, understanding the nuances of language and communication can significantly enhance your experience and interactions with locals. This travel guide aims to provide you with comprehensive insights into the linguistic landscape of Croatia, covering the official language, regional dialects, and cultural communication norms. Whether you are strolling through the cobbled streets of Dubrovnik, exploring the historical wonders of Split, or unwinding on the idyllic islands, a basic grasp of the local language will undoubtedly enrich your journey.

1. Official Language and Regional Dialects

1.1 Croatian Language: Hrvatski

The official and most widely spoken language in Croatia is Croatian (Hrvatski). Croatian is a South

Slavic language, belonging to the Indo-European language family. It uses the Latin script with a few additional diacritical marks on certain letters, which can impact pronunciation. For travelers with a background in English or other Romance languages, Croatian may present some linguistic similarities, making it somewhat easier to learn basic phrases.

1.2 Regional Variations

While standard Croatian is understood throughout the country, various regional dialects add charm and diversity to Croatia's linguistic landscape. Some prominent regional variations include:

1.2.1 Istrian Dialect: Spoken in the Istrian Peninsula, this dialect exhibits influences from Italian and Slovenian due to its geographical proximity to Italy and Slovenia.

1.2.2 Dalmatian Dialect: Found in the Dalmatian region, this dialect features unique intonations and pronunciation that differ from the standard Croatian.

1.2.3 Dubrovnik Dialect: Dubrovnik, a cultural gem, has its own distinct dialect, characterized by archaic words and phrases, making it a fascinating linguistic pocket.

2. Useful Phrases and Expressions

As you embark on your Croatian adventure, having a grasp of some essential phrases and expressions will go a long way in fostering connections with locals and navigating day-to-day situations:

2.1 Greetings and Polite Expressions:
- Hello: Bok (informal) / Dobar dan (formal)
- Goodbye: Doviđenja
- Please: Molim
- Thank you: Hvala
- You're welcome: Nema na čemu
- Excuse me: Oprostite
- Sorry: Žao mi je

2.2 Basic Conversational Phrases:
- Yes: Da
- No: Ne
- What is your name?: Kako se zovete? (formal) / Kako se zoveš? (informal)
- My name is...: Zovem se...
- How are you?: Kako ste? (formal) / Kako si? (informal)
- I'm fine, thank you: Dobro sam, hvala.
- I don't understand: Ne razumijem.
- Can you help me?: Možete li mi pomoći?

3. *Language Etiquette and Cultural Communication*

3.1 Addressing Locals

When communicating with locals, it's essential to be mindful of formal and informal modes of address. Croatians generally appreciate polite language and the use of formal pronouns when addressing strangers, older individuals, or those in positions of authority. The formal "vi" is used for addressing someone with respect, while the informal "ti" is used with friends or peers.

3.2 Non-Verbal Communication

Like in many cultures, non-verbal communication plays a significant role in Croatia. Maintaining eye contact during conversations is a sign of respect and engagement. Handshakes are a common form of greeting, especially in more formal settings. When meeting someone for the first time, a warm and firm handshake is appropriate.

3.3 Cultural Sensitivity

Croatians take pride in their traditions, history, and language. While discussing sensitive topics like politics, war, or religion, it's essential to approach them with respect and sensitivity. Engaging in cultural discussions can foster understanding, but it's best to be mindful of potential sensitivities.

4. Language Learning Resources

4.1 Language Apps and Websites

Before embarking on your Croatian journey, consider using language learning apps and websites to familiarize yourself with the basics. Apps like Duolingo, Babbel, and Memrise offer interactive lessons and exercises tailored for beginners.

4.2 Language Classes and Language Exchanges

If you prefer in-person learning, language classes are available in many Croatian cities, catering to tourists. Additionally, language exchange events are a great way to practice with locals who want to improve their English while helping you with your Croatian.

Croatia is a land of breathtaking landscapes, intriguing history, and warm hospitality. By embracing the local language and communication norms, you will undoubtedly forge deeper connections with the people and the culture. While many Croatians speak English and are eager to assist tourists, making an effort to communicate in their native language will be greatly appreciated and leave a lasting impression. So, as you explore the picturesque towns, ancient ruins, and pristine beaches, immerse yourself in the beauty of the Croatian language and enjoy the unforgettable experiences it brings to your journey.

•Safety and Emergency Information

Croatia is a breathtaking destination that offers a diverse range of experiences, from historic cities and beautiful coastlines to stunning national parks and charming villages. However, as with any travel destination, it is essential for travelers to be aware of safety and emergency information to ensure a pleasant and trouble-free trip. This comprehensive guide will provide vital insights into staying safe while exploring the wonders of Croatia in various situations, from general travel safety tips to specific emergency protocols.

I. General Travel Safety Tips

1. Travel Insurance: Before embarking on your journey to Croatia, it is highly recommended to purchase comprehensive travel insurance that covers medical emergencies, trip cancellations, and personal belongings.

2. Register with Your Embassy: Register your travel plans with your country's embassy in Croatia. This allows your government to assist you in case of emergencies or unforeseen situations.

3. Stay Informed: Stay updated on current travel advisories and safety warnings issued by your government. This information can help you make

informed decisions and stay away from potentially dangerous areas.

4. Be Wary of Scams: As with any tourist destination, be vigilant of common scams, such as pickpocketing, fake taxi services, and overpriced goods. Always use licensed taxis and be cautious when sharing personal information with strangers.

5. Respect Local Customs: Familiarize yourself with Croatia's cultural norms and etiquette to avoid unintentionally offending locals.

II. Transportation Safety

1. Road Safety: If you plan on driving in Croatia, be aware of local traffic regulations and road conditions. Roads can be winding and narrow in certain areas, so drive cautiously, especially in rural regions.

2. Public Transport: Croatia has a well-developed public transportation system, including buses and ferries. Utilize these services, especially if you are not accustomed to driving in a foreign country.

3. Taxi Safety: Only use registered taxis with visible identification and meters. Negotiate the fare before starting your journey.

4. Maritime Safety: If you plan to explore the beautiful Croatian islands, ensure you choose reputable ferry services with a good safety record.

III. Outdoor Activities and Natural Hazards

1. Beach Safety: Croatia's coastline is renowned for its crystal-clear waters and beautiful beaches. However, it is crucial to adhere to beach safety guidelines, including respecting lifeguards' warnings, swimming within designated areas, and avoiding risky behaviors in the water.

2. Hiking and Nature Trails: Croatia offers numerous hiking and nature trails, particularly in its national parks. Always stick to marked paths, wear appropriate footwear, and bring plenty of water and snacks.

3. Sun Protection: Croatia experiences a Mediterranean climate, and the sun can be intense, especially during the summer months. Use sunscreen, wear a hat, and stay hydrated to avoid heat-related illnesses.

4. Forest Fire Prevention: During the dry season, there is an increased risk of forest fires. Pay attention to fire hazard warnings and avoid activities that could cause wildfires, such as lighting fires or discarding cigarette butts carelessly.

IV. Health and Medical Facilities

1. Vaccinations and Health Precautions: Before traveling to Croatia, check with your healthcare provider regarding recommended vaccinations and health precautions.

2. Medical Facilities: Croatia has well-equipped medical facilities in major cities and tourist areas. If you need medical assistance, head to the nearest hospital or medical clinic.

3. Prescription Medications: If you require prescription medications, bring an adequate supply for the duration of your trip and carry a copy of the prescription or a doctor's note.

V. Emergency Contacts

In case of emergencies, these are the important contact numbers to keep handy:

1. Medical Emergencies: Dial 112 for an ambulance or head directly to the nearest hospital.

2. Police: Dial 192 to report a crime or seek assistance from the police.

3. Fire Department: Dial 193 to report a fire or request firefighting services.

4. National Search and Rescue: Dial 195 to seek assistance in search and rescue situations.

Croatia is a captivating destination that promises unforgettable experiences to travelers. By following the safety and emergency information provided in this guide, you can ensure a smooth and enjoyable journey. Stay informed, exercise caution, and be respectful of local customs to make the most of your visit to this enchanting country. With the right preparation, you can explore Croatia's natural beauty, history, and culture while keeping yourself and your fellow travelers safe and secure.

•Local Customs and Etiquette

Croatia, a breathtaking country nestled in the Balkans, offers travelers a unique blend of history, natural beauty, and vibrant culture. As you embark on your journey through this enchanting land, understanding the local customs and etiquette will enhance your experience and ensure that you leave a positive impression on the locals. In this comprehensive Croatia travel guide, we delve into the rich tapestry of Croatian customs, traditions, and social norms to help you navigate your way through the country with grace and respect.

1. Greetings and Introductions:

Croatians value warm and respectful greetings. When meeting someone for the first time, a handshake is a common gesture, while close friends and family may exchange hugs or cheek kisses. Addressing people with their titles (Mr., Mrs., Miss) followed by their last names is considered polite. Croatians often use "Dobar dan" (Good day) as a standard greeting throughout the day. In the evening, you can switch to "Dobra večer" (Good evening).

2. *Dress Code:*

Croatians generally take pride in their appearance, and dressing well is appreciated, especially in urban areas and more formal settings. For visiting churches, cathedrals, or other religious sites, modest attire is expected, with shoulders and knees covered. On the beaches and in coastal areas, casual and beachwear is acceptable.

3. *Dining Etiquette:*

Croatian cuisine is a delightful fusion of Mediterranean and Central European influences, and sharing a meal is an essential part of Croatian culture. When invited to someone's home for a meal, it is customary to bring a small gift, such as flowers or wine, to show your appreciation. Dining etiquette dictates that you wait for the host to begin eating before you start your meal. During the meal, keep your hands visible on the table, and remember to say "Prijatno" (Enjoy your meal) after finishing.

4. Tipping:

Tipping in Croatia is not obligatory, as a service charge is usually included in the bill. However, leaving a small tip for good service, especially in restaurants and cafes, is appreciated. A tip of around 10% of the total bill is considered generous.

5. Language:

While English is widely spoken, particularly in tourist areas, learning a few basic Croatian phrases will be greatly appreciated by the locals and can help you connect with them on a more personal level. Simple greetings and thank-you expressions go a long way in making a positive impression.

6. Socializing and Hospitality:

Croatians are renowned for their warm hospitality, and if you are invited into someone's home, you will be treated like an honored guest. Removing your shoes before entering is a common practice in many households. It is polite to bring a small gift for the host, such as chocolates or a souvenir from your home country.

7. Respect for Traditions:

Croatia boasts a rich cultural heritage, and locals take pride in preserving their traditions. When visiting historical sites or participating in cultural events, show respect for the customs and rules. Taking photographs in churches or places of worship may be prohibited, so always look for signs or ask for permission before doing so.

8. Public Behavior:

Croatians value their personal space and tend to maintain a level of formality with strangers. Avoid raising your voice or engaging in loud conversations in public places. It is also essential to be mindful of your surroundings and avoid leaving trash in public areas as cleanliness is highly valued in Croatia.

9. Festivals and Celebrations:

Croatia hosts numerous festivals and events throughout the year, celebrating everything from music and dance to historical reenactments. If you have the opportunity to attend one of these gatherings, immerse yourself in the local culture and participate with enthusiasm. Respect the customs and traditions associated with each celebration.

10. Religion:

Religion plays a significant role in Croatian culture, with the majority of the population being Roman

Catholic. When visiting religious sites, remember to dress modestly and act respectfully. Even if you do not share the same beliefs, be sensitive and observe the customs practiced by the locals.

As you embark on your Croatian adventure, embracing the local customs and etiquette will not only enrich your travel experience but also foster meaningful connections with the hospitable and warm-hearted Croatian people. By showing respect for their traditions, culture, and way of life, you will undoubtedly leave a positive and lasting impression on this mesmerizing Balkan nation. Embrace the beauty of Croatia, savor its delicious cuisine, and cherish the memories you create by immersing yourself in the customs and etiquettes of this enchanting country.

CHAPTER NINE

Sustainable Travel and Responsible Tourism

•*Eco-Friendly Practices in Croatia*

Croatia, a jewel on the Adriatic Sea, is renowned for its stunning coastline, ancient cities, and rich cultural heritage. As tourism continues to play a significant role in Croatia's economy, there has been an increasing awareness of the need to adopt eco-friendly practices to preserve the country's natural beauty and cultural treasures for future generations. In recent years, Croatia has made significant strides in promoting sustainable tourism and encouraging visitors to adopt environmentally responsible behaviors. This comprehensive travel guide aims to shed light on the eco-friendly practices and initiatives in Croatia, enabling travelers to make conscientious choices while exploring this breathtaking country.

1. Preservation of Natural Resources:

One of the primary focuses of Croatia's eco-friendly initiatives lies in preserving its abundant natural resources, particularly its stunning coastline and crystal-clear waters. The country's national parks and protected areas are strictly monitored to prevent overtourism and ecosystem degradation. Tourists are encouraged to follow designated paths and refrain from littering or disturbing wildlife.

2. *Sustainable Accommodation Options:*

Croatia offers an array of eco-friendly accommodation options to suit all budgets. Many hotels and guesthouses have adopted sustainable practices, such as energy-efficient lighting, water-saving measures, and waste recycling programs. Additionally, eco-lodges and agrotourism establishments provide a unique opportunity to experience Croatia's countryside while supporting local communities that practice sustainable farming.

3. *Promoting Public Transportation and Cycling:*

To reduce the environmental impact of transportation, Croatia encourages visitors to use public transportation options whenever possible. Cities like Zagreb, Split, and Dubrovnik have well-developed public transportation systems, making it convenient for travelers to explore the urban areas without relying on cars. Moreover, Croatia's diverse landscapes make it an ideal destination for cycling enthusiasts, with numerous bike rental services and well-marked cycling routes available.

4. Local and Organic Cuisine:

Exploring the flavors of Croatia is a delightful experience that also supports sustainable practices. Many restaurants and eateries in Croatia prioritize locally sourced and organic ingredients, reducing food miles and supporting local farmers and producers. Embracing the farm-to-table concept, these establishments offer fresh and authentic Croatian dishes with minimal ecological impact.

5. Responsible Sailing and Boating:

With its beautiful coastline and numerous islands, Croatia is a popular destination for sailing and boating enthusiasts. To protect the marine ecosystem, travelers are encouraged to participate in responsible boating practices. This includes avoiding dropping anchor in protected areas, adhering to speed limits, and properly disposing of waste to prevent pollution of the sea.

6. Eco-Friendly Activities:

Croatia offers an abundance of eco-friendly activities that allow travelers to immerse themselves in the country's natural beauty while respecting the environment. Hiking and trekking in national parks like Plitvice Lakes or Krka

Waterfalls, birdwatching in wetland reserves, and participating in beach clean-up initiatives are just a few examples of eco-friendly activities available.

7. Cultural Preservation and Respect:

Preserving Croatia's rich cultural heritage is essential in sustainable tourism. Travelers are encouraged to respect historical sites, museums, and local customs. When visiting traditional villages and local communities, engaging with residents in a respectful and responsible manner ensures a positive impact on both visitors and locals.

8. Waste Reduction and Recycling:

To combat the challenges of waste management and pollution, Croatia has been investing in recycling programs and initiatives to minimize plastic and other non-biodegradable waste. Visitors are urged to support these efforts by reducing their plastic consumption, using reusable water bottles, and properly disposing of waste in designated recycling bins.

Croatia's commitment to eco-friendly practices and sustainable tourism makes it an exemplary destination for conscientious travelers seeking to explore nature's wonders and immerse themselves in a rich cultural heritage. By embracing eco-friendly accommodation, responsible transportation, and engaging in sustainable activities, visitors can play an active role in preserving Croatia's pristine landscapes and unique cultural treasures for generations to come. Let this eco-friendly travel guide be your compass as you embark on an unforgettable and sustainable journey through Croatia's breathtaking landscapes and vibrant traditions.

•*Supporting Local Communities*

Croatia is a gem nestled in the heart of Europe, boasting breathtaking coastlines, historic cities, charming villages, and a rich cultural heritage. While the country has become an increasingly popular travel destination, it is essential to consider the impact of tourism on local communities. Responsible tourism practices and supporting local communities are crucial for preserving the country's natural beauty and ensuring the sustainability of its cultural heritage. In this travel guide, we will explore ways to support local communities in Croatia while enjoying a memorable and authentic experience.

1. *Understanding the Importance of Supporting Local Communities*

Croatia's local communities are the backbone of its unique identity and charm. Engaging with locals and supporting their livelihoods not only enhances your travel experience but also contributes positively to the preservation of Croatian traditions and heritage. Tourism can bring both opportunities and challenges to local communities, and it's our responsibility as travelers to foster sustainable practices.

2. Opting for Locally Owned Accommodations

When choosing accommodation in Croatia, consider staying in locally-owned hotels, guesthouses, or private rentals. These establishments are more likely to reinvest their earnings into the community, providing job opportunities and economic growth. Furthermore, they often offer an authentic experience, allowing you to immerse yourself in the local culture and customs.

3. Embracing Local Cuisine and Products

Croatia boasts a diverse culinary scene, with each region offering its unique dishes and flavors. To support local communities, opt for restaurants and eateries that use locally sourced ingredients and traditional recipes. By doing so, you not only savor delicious meals but also contribute to the preservation of traditional farming practices and the livelihoods of local producers.

4. Participating in Local Events and Festivals

Croatia is renowned for its vibrant festivals and events, celebrating everything from music and art to food and wine. Attending these local gatherings not only offers an unforgettable experience but also supports local artisans, musicians, and vendors. Additionally, your presence as a traveler helps promote the continuity of these events for generations to come.

5. Engaging in Responsible Tourism

Responsible tourism involves being mindful of the environment, culture, and society. When exploring Croatia's natural wonders, such as its national parks and coastlines, follow designated trails, avoid littering, and opt for eco-friendly activities like hiking, kayaking, or snorkeling. By being conscious of your impact, you help preserve Croatia's stunning landscapes for future generations.

6. Supporting Local Arts and Crafts

Croatia has a rich artistic heritage, encompassing traditional crafts such as pottery, embroidery, and wood carving. Seek out local artisans and workshops to purchase authentic handmade souvenirs, supporting their skills and craftsmanship. These items not only carry a piece of

Croatia's cultural legacy but also make for meaningful and sustainable mementos of your trip.

7. Engaging with Local Social Enterprises

Throughout Croatia, various social enterprises focus on empowering local communities, especially those facing economic challenges. These initiatives often involve local products, such as handcrafted goods or organic produce. By supporting these enterprises, you contribute to social development and the preservation of traditional knowledge and skills.

8. Volunteering and Community Initiatives

For travelers seeking a deeper connection with Croatia, consider volunteering with local community projects. From environmental conservation efforts to educational initiatives, there are numerous opportunities to give back to the places you visit. Volunteering not only supports the local community directly but also enriches your travel experience by creating meaningful interactions with locals.

9. Learning the Language and Customs

A genuine effort to learn a few basic Croatian phrases and respect local customs can go a long way in forging connections with the people you meet. Locals will appreciate your willingness to engage with their language and culture, making your interactions more meaningful and enjoyable.

10. Spreading the Word

Lastly, as a responsible traveler, share your experiences and knowledge of supporting local communities in Croatia with others. By raising awareness of sustainable tourism practices, you contribute to a more responsible and conscious travel culture that benefits both travelers and the local communities they visit.

Croatia's beauty and charm extend beyond its picturesque landscapes; it lies within the warmth and hospitality of its local communities. As travelers, it is our duty to ensure that our presence enhances their lives and preserves their cultural heritage for generations to come. By supporting local communities in Croatia, we not only create memorable travel experiences but also foster sustainable tourism practices that protect this precious destination. So, pack your bags, embrace the Croatian spirit, and embark on a journey that leaves a positive impact on the places and people you encounter along the way.

CHAPTER TEN

Useful Phrases and Vocabulary

•*Basic Croatian Phrases for Travelers*

Croatia, a stunning country in southeastern Europe, is a popular travel destination known for its breathtaking coastlines, historic cities, rich culture, and warm hospitality. While English is widely spoken in tourist areas, learning some basic Croatian phrases can enhance your travel experience and show respect for the local culture. This guide aims to provide travelers with essential Croatian phrases to help them navigate through the country, interact with locals, and immerse themselves in the unique Croatian way of life.

1. *Greetings and Polite Expressions:*

Learning a few greetings and polite expressions in Croatian can go a long way in making a positive impression and creating a friendly atmosphere during your travels:

1. Dobar dan (DOH-bahr dahn) - Good day / Hello (used during the day)

2. Dobro jutro (DOH-broh YOO-troh) - Good morning
3. Dobra večer (DOH-brah VEH-chehr) - Good evening
4. Hvala (HVAH-lah) - Thank you
5. Molim (MOH-leem) - Please / You're welcome (when someone thanks you)
6. Oprostite (oh-PROHS-tee-teh) - Excuse me / I'm sorry
7. Da (dah) - Yes
8. Ne (neh) - No
9. Hvala lijepa (HVAH-lah LEE-yeh-pah) - Thank you very much
10. Bok (bohk) - Bye

2. Basic Communication:

Navigating daily interactions becomes easier when you know how to ask basic questions and understand common responses:

1. Kako se zovete? (KAH-koh seh ZOH-veh-teh) - What is your name?
2. Zovem se (your name) (ZOH-vehm seh) - My name is (your name)
3. Govorite li engleski? (GOH-voh-ree-teh lee EHN-glehs-kee) - Do you speak English?
4. Ne razumijem (neh rah-ZOO-mee-yem) - I don't understand
5. Molim vas, možete li mi pomoći? (MOH-leem vahs, MOH-zheh-teh lee mee POH-moh-chee) - Can you help me, please?

6. Koliko košta? (KOH-lee-koh KOH-shta) - How much does it cost?
7. Gdje je WC? (gdyeh yeh vay-tsay) - Where is the restroom?

3. Getting Around:

When traveling in Croatia, knowing how to ask for directions and transportation options can be beneficial:

1. Gdje je željeznički kolodvor? (gdyeh yeh ZHEHL-yehz-neech-kee KOH-lohd-vohr) - Where is the train station?
2. Gdje je autobusni kolodvor? (gdyeh yeh OW-toh-boos-nee KOH-lohd-vohr) - Where is the bus station?
3. Kako mogu doći do hotela (hotel name)? (KAH-koh MOH-goo doh-chee doh hoh-TEHL) - How can I get to the hotel (hotel name)?
4. Koliko košta karta? (KOH-lee-koh KOH-shta KAHR-tah) - How much is the ticket?
5. Vozi li ovaj autobus/ vlak za (your destination)? (VOH-zee lee oh-vai OW-vai vlahk zah) - Does this bus/train go to (your destination)?

4. Ordering Food and Drinks:

Sampling delicious Croatian cuisine is a must for any traveler. Here's how to order food and drinks:

1. Konobar (male waiter) / Konobarica (female waiter) (KOH-noh-bahr / KOH-noh-bah-ree-tsah) - Waiter / Waitress
2. Hladno/piće (HLAH-dnoh/PEE-cheh) - Cold drink
3. Voda (VOH-dah) - Water
4. Pivo (PEE-voh) - Beer
5. Vino (VEE-noh) - Wine
6. Jelo (YEH-loh) - Food / Meal
7. Račun, molim (RAH-choon, MOH-leem) - The check, please
8. Gdje mogu jesti dobru hranu? (gdyeh MOH-goo YEHS-tee DOH-broo HRAH-noo) - Where can I eat good food?

5. Emergency Phrases:

While Croatia is generally a safe country for travelers, knowing a few emergency phrases is essential:

1. Pomoć! (POH-mohtch) - Help!
2. Hitna pomoć (HEET-nah POH-mohtch) - Emergency help
3. Policija (poh-LEE-tsyah) - Police
4. Bolje mi je (BOH-lyeh mee yeh) - I am feeling better

Mastering some basic Croatian phrases can significantly enhance your travel experience in Croatia and foster meaningful connections with the locals. While many Croatians speak English, making an effort to communicate in their native language will be appreciated and show respect for their culture. As you explore the beautiful landscapes, ancient cities, and charming villages of Croatia, don't hesitate to use these phrases and immerse yourself in the country's vibrant culture and warm hospitality.

•*Food and Restaurant Vocabulary*

In this comprehensive Croatia travel guide, we will dive into the world of Croatian food and restaurant vocabulary, helping you navigate local menus and understand traditional dishes. Get ready to savor the flavors of Croatia and embrace the culinary delights that await you.

1. Croatian Gastronomy - A Fusion of Traditions

Croatian cuisine is a delightful amalgamation of diverse influences from neighboring countries and regions, each contributing its own unique flair. From coastal cities to mountainous regions, every area boasts its culinary specialty. Here are some essential terms to familiarize yourself with when diving into Croatian gastronomy:

1.1 Hrana (Food) and Jelo (Dish)

In Croatian, "hrana" means food, and "jelo" refers to a dish or a meal. These two words are the essence of what you will experience in Croatia.

1.2 Riblji Restoran (Fish Restaurant) and Morski Plodovi (Seafood)

Croatia's long coastline and proximity to the Adriatic Sea make seafood a highlight of the local cuisine. A "riblji restoran" is a fish restaurant, and "morski plodovi" denotes a variety of seafood delicacies.

1.3 Meso (Meat) and Mesnica (Butcher Shop)

For meat lovers, "meso" is an important term to remember. Additionally, a "mesnica" is a butcher shop where you can purchase fresh cuts of meat.

2. Essential Croatian Dishes

As you explore Croatia, you'll encounter several iconic dishes that are staples of the local food scene. Understanding their names will help you make informed choices while dining:

2.1 Peka

Peka is a traditional Croatian dish prepared under a bell-like dome, which is buried in hot ashes. This cooking method allows the flavors of meat or seafood, vegetables, and aromatic herbs to blend perfectly.

2.2 Crni Rižot (Black Risotto)

This unique dish gets its dark color from cuttlefish ink, giving the risotto a rich seafood flavor. It's a must-try for seafood enthusiasts.

2.3 Ćevapi (Grilled Minced Meat)
Ćevapi are small, skinless sausages made from minced meat, typically a mix of beef, lamb, and pork. Served with traditional flatbread called "lepinja" and diced onions, it's a popular street food.

2.4 Palačinke (Croatian Pancakes)
Palačinke are thin, crepe-like pancakes often filled with sweet fillings like jam, chocolate, or nuts, but they can also be savory, filled with cheese, ham, or spinach.

3. Croatian Restaurant Vocabulary

To enhance your dining experience in Croatia, familiarize yourself with some essential restaurant vocabulary:

3.1 Dobrodošli (Welcome)
Upon entering a restaurant, you'll likely be greeted with "Dobrodošli," which means welcome.

3.2 Meni (Menu) and Dnevni Meni (Daily Menu)
When you are ready to order, ask for the "meni" (menu) or inquire about the "dnevni meni" (daily menu) for fresh, seasonal dishes.

3.3 Predjelo (Appetizer) and Glavno Jelo (Main Course)
Croatian cuisine often includes a variety of appetizers, known as "predjelo," and hearty main courses, referred to as "glavno jelo."

3.4 Piće (Drink) and Vino (Wine)
Quench your thirst with a refreshing "piće" (drink) or opt for a delightful glass of Croatian wine, "vino."

3.5 Račun (Bill) and Napojnica (Tip)
When you're ready to settle the bill, ask for the "račun," and if you've enjoyed your dining experience, you can leave a "napojnica" (tip) for the staff.

4. Dietary Preferences and Special Requests

If you have dietary restrictions or special preferences, it's crucial to communicate them effectively. Here are some phrases to help you express your needs:

4.1 Vegetarijanski (Vegetarian) and Veganski (Vegan)
If you're a vegetarian or vegan, these terms will be useful when discussing dietary preferences.

4.2 Bez Glutena (Gluten-Free) and Bez Laktoze (Lactose-Free)
For those with gluten or lactose intolerance, "bez glutena" and "bez laktoze" are essential phrases.

4.3 Alergija (Allergy) and Alergičan Sam Na (I'm Allergic to)

In case of food allergies, use "alergija" followed by the specific allergen, e.g., "Alergičan sam na kikiriki" (I'm allergic to peanuts).

5. Regional Delicacies

Each region of Croatia boasts its culinary specialties, and you won't want to miss trying them. Here are some noteworthy regional delicacies:

5.1 Istria: Istrian Truffles

The Istrian region is famous for its exquisite truffles. Don't miss the chance to indulge in truffle-infused dishes such as "Fuži s Tartufima" (pasta with truffles) or "Tartufata."

5.2 Dalmatia: Dalmatian Prosciutto and Peka

Dalmatia is known for its mouthwatering prosciutto and the traditional "peka" dishes cooked under a bell.

5.3 Zagreb: Štrukli

When in Zagreb, don't miss trying "štrukli," a delicious pastry filled with cheese, sour cream, or fruit, and often topped with cream.

As you traverse through Croatia, you'll discover that the country's food and restaurant vocabulary are a gateway to its culture and history. Embrace the culinary diversity, try regional delicacies, and immerse yourself in the flavors that have shaped this captivating nation. Whether you're dining in a bustling city restaurant or a charming coastal tavern, understanding the local food lingo will enhance your culinary experience and leave you with unforgettable memories of your time in Croatia. Enjoy your gastronomic journey through this beautiful country!

CHAPTER ELEVEN

•*Conclusion*

Conclusion:

In conclusion, Croatia is a mesmerizing and diverse destination that offers a wealth of experiences for every type of traveler. From its stunning coastline and idyllic islands to its historical cities, lush national parks, and vibrant cultural heritage, Croatia stands out as an unforgettable gem in the heart of Europe. Throughout this comprehensive travel guide, we have explored the various aspects of this beautiful country, highlighting its top attractions, activities, culinary delights, and practical travel tips.

Croatia's Adriatic coast, with its breathtaking beaches, azure waters, and charming coastal towns, is a magnet for beach lovers, water sports enthusiasts, and those seeking relaxation in an enchanting setting. Whether you choose the popular hotspots like Dubrovnik and Split or opt for the more tranquil islands like Hvar or Korčula, the coastal region offers a perfect blend of history, culture, and natural beauty.

Venturing inland, Croatia's cities present a rich tapestry of history and architecture. Zagreb, the capital, showcases a vibrant cultural scene, museums, and a lively atmosphere that captivates visitors. The ancient cities of Zadar, Šibenik, and Trogir boast medieval charm, with their well-preserved historical centers and impressive landmarks like St. James' Cathedral and the Sea Organ in Zadar.

Nature lovers will find their paradise in Croatia's national parks. Plitvice Lakes, with its cascading waterfalls and emerald lakes, is a true wonder of the natural world. Krka National Park, with its magnificent waterfalls and hiking trails, offers an unforgettable escape into nature's beauty. For adventure seekers, Paklenica National Park provides excellent rock climbing and trekking opportunities amid dramatic canyons and rugged cliffs.

Croatia's cultural heritage is equally captivating, with a blend of influences from various civilizations that have left their mark over the centuries. Delving into the country's history reveals Roman ruins, medieval fortresses, and Renaissance palaces. The Diocletian's Palace in Split is a prime example of how history is intricately woven into the fabric of Croatia's present-day life.

As we've highlighted the places to visit and things to do, we must also mention the culinary delights that Croatia has to offer. Its gastronomic scene is a delightful fusion of Mediterranean, Balkan, and

Central European cuisines. From freshly caught seafood and succulent meats to artisanal cheeses and wines, Croatia's culinary offerings are sure to tantalize your taste buds.

Traveling in Croatia is made easier by a well-connected transportation system and a wide range of accommodation options. Whether you prefer luxury resorts, boutique hotels, family-run guesthouses, or budget-friendly hostels, you'll find suitable choices throughout the country. Croatia's warm and welcoming locals add an extra layer of charm, making visitors feel at home and creating unforgettable memories.

To make the most of your trip, it's essential to consider the best time to visit each region. The coastal areas are most popular during the summer months when the weather is warm and the Adriatic Sea beckons for a refreshing swim. However, the shoulder seasons of spring and autumn offer a more peaceful experience, with milder weather and fewer crowds. For those interested in exploring the national parks and inland cities, these transitional periods provide comfortable temperatures for outdoor activities.

While Croatia has made significant strides in developing its tourism industry, it's vital to respect the country's cultural and environmental heritage. As responsible travelers, we should strive to preserve the natural beauty and unique cultural identity of Croatia for future generations to enjoy.

In conclusion, a journey to Croatia promises an adventure that will stay with you long after you've returned home. Its diverse landscapes, rich history, and warm hospitality create an alluring destination that captures the hearts of travelers from around the world. Whether you seek relaxation on sun-kissed shores, an exploration of ancient cities, or an immersion into nature's wonders, Croatia offers it all and more. Embrace the essence of this enchanting country, and you will undoubtedly be rewarded with unforgettable experiences and cherished memories that will last a lifetime. So, pack your bags, embark on an unforgettable journey, and let Croatia weave its magic on your soul. Happy travels!